THE RACE

KYLE FROMAN AND BILLY MAULDIN

THE RACE

LIVING LIFE
ON TRACK WITH
NASCAR HALL-OF-FAMER
DARRELL
WALTRIP

B&H
PUBLISHING GROUP
NASHVILLE, TENNESSEE

978-1-4336-8372-5

Published by B&H Publishing Group
Nashville, Tennessee

Dewey Decimal Classification: 248.842
Subject Heading: CHRISTIAN LIFE \ STOCK CAR
RACING \ MEN

Unless otherwise noted, Scripture quotations are taken from
the Holman Christian Standard Bible®, Copyright © 1999,
2000, 2002, 2003, 2009 by Holman Bible Publishers.

Also used: New International Version (NIV),
copyright © 1973, 1978, 1984 by International Bible Society.
Also used: *The Message*, the New Testament in Contemporary
English, © 1993 by Eugene H. Peterson, published by
NavPress, Colorado Springs, Colorado.

Also used: *The Amplified*® Bible (AMP), Copyright © 1954,
1958, 1962, 1964, 1965, 1987 by The Lockman Foundation
Used by permission. (www.Lockman.org)

1 2 3 4 5 6 7 • 18 17 16 15 14

Dedication

To Our Wives: Julie and Michelle

To Our Children: Thor, Titan, Daisy,
Roxy, Micah, and Kaleb

Acknowledgments

We are thankful for the grace and mercy we receive from our heavenly Father, and the opportunities He has allowed us to be conduits of His truth to those around us. Just as the body of Christ comes together through many different gifts and talents, *The Race* would not have been published without the contributions of an amazing team behind us. To Darrell and Stevie Waltrip, thank you for living your lives in such a way that is pleasing to the Lord, and for bringing your experiences to *The Race*. To Dawn Woods, Laurel Teague, Kim Stanford, Jason Ellerbrook, and the rest of the B&H Publishing and Lifeway team, thank you for your extensive efforts to help us share this message. You believed lives would be transformed by *The Race*, and we are thankful you have supported the project. To the staff of Motor Racing Outreach, past and present, you are the heart of the message we share. Thank you for living your lives in such a way that would illuminate and elevate God in the world of motor sports. Max, you led the way! To the community we serve, thank you for allowing us to be a part of your lives and to live out the principles that we've shared in *The Race*. To Rusty Shelton and the Shelton Interactive team, thank you for your expertise in advancing the message of *The Race*. To our parents, thank you for pouring into us and pointing us towards truth in our lives. We are thankful to each and every person who has their fingerprint on *The Race*.

Contents

Section 1

Preparing for Mission

Chapter 1

Before You Hit the Track

Be Prepared

"Teams put in the long, hard hours on the front end because they know if it's not right when they get to the track, it can sometimes be almost impossible to get the car to the winner's circle."

From Darrell Waltrip

Preparation is everything if you want to be competitive and win a lot of races in this sport. You hear it said all the time: the work is done in the shop. It takes a large group of people coming together there, putting in the hours and the sweat, to become a competitive team. They put in the long, hard hours on the front end because they know if it's not right when they get to the track, it can sometimes be almost impossible to get the car to the winner's circle. The team's goal, week in and week out, is to unload with a well-prepared, win-worthy race car so that when the driver straps in for practice, all that's left is minor tweaks and adjustments.

Back in the day, our race team was a small band of generalists. We were a group of twelve to fifteen guys who did all the work on the car—from fabrications to set-ups, all our hands were in the pot. After preparing the car back at the shop, the same group of twelve to fifteen would load everything up and travel to the race together.

Even though we were a small team, we were meticulous. My cars looked slick each and every time I went to the racetrack; I always insisted they be flawless. From the beginning, I felt that how we prepared our cars and how they looked when we got to the track was a reflection of who we were as a team. There was no excuse to arrive at the track with a dirty, careless, unprepared car. I hold to this standard to this day!

Today, we see a shift in the size of race teams. What used to be a small band of generalists preparing cars at the shop and traveling with them on the road has turned into large teams of specialists. Every facet of that race car—from the engine, transmission, and running gear to the set-up, body, and interior—has specialists dedicated to making sure it is perfect and who focus in on just that facet. So in the past, where we were a small group of people who were good at every-thing, now there is a large team of people with very specific jobs that they are trained to do. Their expertise becomes their focus, and they really don't do anything else on the team.

At the shop, a car essentially begins as a pile of metal. The process of transforming the metal into a race car starts on the frame rack, or jig, in the chassis shop, with chassis specialists devoted to bringing the race car to life. Beginning with two frame rails, the specialists add the front clip, rear clip, and roll cage to round out the chassis. The race car then gets rolled out to the body shop, where a team of fabrication special-ists meticulously craft the body that is to be hung on the completed chassis. The body itself is a work of art, handcrafted to fit the myriad of NASCAR templates the car will run through.

After the body shop, the car will go to the set-up shop where the teams who specialize in gears, brakes, suspensions, and more will get busy. Meanwhile, over in the engine room, another team of experts works on the power plant that will drive the car down the track. As the set-up team finishes, the built and tuned engine will be lowered into the car, then wired and connected into place. Finally, the finishing touches to the interior will be finalized and the body will be wrapped with the team colors.

So everything happens before the car ever gets to the track. By the time we load the race car into the hauler and roll off to the next track, all the hard work is done. The hopeful end result is that the driver is happy and that the race car is fast, ultimately bringing home the hardware at the end of the race.

From Kyle Froman

There is a scene in an old racing movie, *Days of Thunder*, where two racers who are bitter rivals are forced to go to dinner together in the same car. Neither will allow the other to drive, so they rent a second car. What ensues is a classic Hollywood race scene in which these two guys duke it out through the streets—bumper to bumper and fender to fender—the whole way to their destination. Upon arrival, they leave their battered, smoking, wrecked rental cars with the valet and proceed inside.

Neither racer was willing to finish second to the other; it's the racer's way.

Winning is in every racer's blood. Whether the driver is pushing himself to cross the finish line in first place or jockeying to get ahead of the next car on the interstate, he will do whatever it takes to finish ahead of everyone else if you put him into something with four wheels.

We, too, are racers. We are in the middle of the greatest race known to mankind: life. Deep down, we are all driven to win. We want to live life in a way that, when we reach our finish line, we can be proud of what we've accomplished. We want to leave a legacy for our family and friends. We want to be remembered for the things we completed. And if we are a follower of Christ, we want to hear the words, "Well done, My good and faithful servant."

From career choices to hobbies, academia to arts and sports, there are so many things we can do with our lives. How in the world are we supposed to define what winning really is? Is it the car parked in the driveway or the number of zeros at the end of our bank account? Is it the palace on the hill or the title on our business card?

As followers of Christ we are commanded to run our race on mission. As we live our lives, we need to run the race and find our way to the victory lane by testifying about the gospel of God's grace (Acts 20:24). This isn't just the way pastors, evangelists, chaplains, and missionaries win; this is what each and every follower of Christ should strive for.

Jesus told His disciples that they were "the salt of the earth" and "the light of the world" (Matt. 5:13–14). He did not suggest to them that they may want to be salt and light to the community around them; He told them they *were* salt and light.

Then, on the night of Jesus' arrest, He prayed, "As you sent Me into the world, I also have sent them into the world" (John 17:18). Following His death and resurrection, Jesus told His disciples, "Peace to you! As the Father has sent Me, I also send you" (John 20:21).

And let's not forget Jesus' directive to His followers before His ascension: "Go, therefore, and make disciples of all nations, baptizing them in the name of the Father and of the Son and of the Holy Spirit, teaching them to observe everything I have commanded you" (Matt. 28:19–20).

Mission isn't merely a suggestion if you love Jesus. Mission is the very essence of what we are commanded to do as followers of Christ. Jesus did not waver in His directive for us to be His ambassadors; being His disciples and living on mission were inseparable. We are all called to testify to the gospel of God's grace. This is how we win. We should all strive to run our race so as to win.

As any competitive racer knows, winning begins back at the shop. As Darrell Waltrip has said, "If it's not right when you get it to the track, sometimes it's almost impossible to get it right." We cannot expect to run a good race unprepared. Many of our successes and failures in life can be traced to our preparation, or lack thereof. A race team cannot show up at a racetrack and unload a pile of metal expecting to win the race. Likewise, we cannot reasonably expect to live our life on mission without preparing for it.

Preparation has always been challenging for me. Let's be real—there are plenty of things we can do with our time that are a lot more exciting than taking the time to prepare. I have yet to walk through a library and hear elation from students who are studying for their next exam. I've not yet had a conversation with a crew member who was eager to work countless hours of overtime to prepare for a race.

The spoils of victory are thrilling. Walking across the stage to receive your diploma, or hoisting the trophy over your head in victory lane, is what it's all about. Preparation? That's the hard stuff. That's where you weed out the winners—by how much work they are willing to do "back at the shop."

I first began to wrestle with the concept of preparation as I headed into eighth grade. In elementary and middle school I was your model, studious student. My lack of athleticism and very small circle of friends afforded me plenty of time to study, complete school-work, and generally excel scholastically. My grades were always a positive reflection of this.

As I transitioned to high school and my hormones morphed, I began to long for a sense of belonging among my peers. Since I didn't have athletics to wow people with, I began to put myself out there in other ways to win friends; I became that guy who would do the stupid things you told him to do just to get a laugh.

The more time I spent making new friends, the less time I spent studying. After investing all my after-school time making friends, I would often set my alarm for 4:00 a.m. on test days so I could wake up early and cram for tests. Unfortunately, alarm clocks have snooze buttons, and teenagers like to sleep, so nine times out of ten, 4:00 a.m. would turn into 6:30 a.m. and I would head to school completely unprepared.

In my quest to make friends, one of the "cool kids" asked me to hang out with him one afternoon after school—when I should have been focusing on school-work. Since I didn't have enough social status to say no, I hung out with him at a lot in our neighborhood where a new house was being built. We passed the time by shattering the construction workers' leftover glass bottles on the cinder-block foundation and half-constructed walls of the home. We'd throw the bottles and dodge whatever liquid was in them as they splashed everywhere.

Since we were doing this in the middle of the day, on a fairly busy street, it did not take long for the neighbors to notice. As I watched a police cruiser pull into that dusty lot, I froze, clenching a dirty, glass Coca-Cola bottle in my hand. I had never been caught on the wrong side of the law before, and I think my heart stopped momentarily as the car halted only a few feet from where I was standing. The officer began to open his door. Trying to catch my breath and wrap my mind around what was happening, I turned to say something to my friend, and all I saw was his trail of dust. He ran. Like the wind. Some "friend" he was. As for me, I was given a "courtesy" ride home.

I will never forget seeing my dad on our riding lawn mower as the cruiser pulled up our long driveway with me in the backseat. My dad smiled and waved as I sat there with tears welling up in my eyes. I watched in horror as the policeman exited the car and slowly walked across the yard to my dad. My dad's smile vanished as he discovered the real reason I was in the back of that car. When he looked back at me again, I buried my head in my hands.

I should have stuck with studying that afternoon, preparing for the next test. Instead, I decided to misuse my time. I would venture to say I didn't make my 4:00 a.m. wake-up call the next morning to study either.

I didn't win that one, but how could I expect to? I didn't prepare!

In the end, my fun translated into something not-so-fun when report cards came home. Instead of cashing in with straight A's, my lack of preparation left me with some explaining to do!

Chad Knaus, crew chief for NASCAR Sprint Cup Series champion Jimmie Johnson, knows that fun doesn't win the race. Preparation does. Just prior to winning his third straight championship, Marty Smith wrote this of Chad: "While others vacation or take a holiday, Knaus is at the shop, holed up in his office viewing tapes of old races and analyzing decisions made, strategizing new ways to outsmart his rivals. The fear of being beaten due to a lack of preparation consumes him."

Now at the peak of his profession, he stands four races from history. Everything he has ever worked for would be validated . . .

. . . So what then? Celebratory vacation?

"That would be really cool," Knaus said. "But it'd be time to go for four."[1]

Chad's passion for preparation led his team to a record-setting five consecutive NASCAR Sprint Cup Series championships. Chad could have rested after championship number one, but his fear of being beaten due to a lack of preparation continued to push him and his team to new heights of success.

In our race, preparation is up to us. We cannot expect to run a good race unprepared any more than Chad Knaus could have won five straight championships with Jimmie Johnson without putting in the blood, sweat, and tears.

Preparation is everything. So the question becomes, how are we preparing to run our race?

In 1 Corinthians 9, Paul recognized the importance of preparation in our race as he wrote:

> Don't you know that the runners in a stadium
> all race, but only one receives the prize? Run in
> such a way to win the prize. Now everyone who

competes exercises self-control in everything. However, they do it to receive a crown that will fade away, but we a crown that will never fade away. Therefore I do not run like one who runs aimlessly or box like one beating the air. Instead, I discipline my body and bring it under strict control, so that after preaching to others, I myself will not be disqualified. (vv. 24–27)

Paul drew a comparison to the Isthmian games, similar to the Olympics, which were a source of pride to the Corinthians.[2] The Corinthians understood the amount of training that went into the games. As fans and possibly participants, they knew that the winning runners did not show up to compete without having endured strict training and discipline prior to the race. They knew an unprepared runner couldn't expect to win.

As we live out the Great Commission of a life on mission, we have to be prepared. Without having put in the time at the shop, there's no point in showing up at the track, because we won't win.

For me and the rest of the Motor Racing Outreach (MRO) team, our race is literally being run at racetracks around the nation. We are living out our lives with a community of people who may or may not be followers of Christ. We face unexpected situations and sudden trauma on a regular basis. We sacrifice time from our loving, supportive families to be out on the road. At any time, we could be called upon to defend the gospel or to lead a wayward soul to truth. Being unprepared in our race would be reckless and potentially embarrassing to ourselves, our families, and those we serve.

In auto racing, drivers can be quickly identified by the name over their door. On one hot summer evening I was making my way down the front straightaway of the Nashville Fairgrounds Speedway, praying with the field of drivers in a now-defunct regional racing series that I had recently begun serving. Since this was only the third race of the season, I was still learning names and faces, so I was relying on the names that were over the drivers' windows as I reached into each car to pray with each driver.

Nearing the end of the field of competitors, I did with the latest car as I had done with all the previous cars: I glanced at the name over the door, leaned in the window to greet the driver, and prayed over him, mentioning his name a few times. As I said, "Amen," and made eye contact with this particular driver, he gave me an uncomfortable, awkward glance.

I then approached the next car and glanced again at the name over the window. That's when it hit me: this one displayed the same name as the previous car. Realizing I'd made an embarrassing mistake, I quickly adjusted my terminology with this next mystery driver, using the word *friend* instead of a name. Still, I felt sick at my error. Simply put, I was unprepared and did not fully know the community I was serving, and it showed.

Our effectiveness in ministry can be directly traced to the amount of our preparation. The spiritual and physical work we put into running our race beforehand will define how well we are able to run. If we aren't prepared when we begin to race, it may be impossible to adjust enough to win.

First, we have to prepare ourselves spiritually.

Recently I had the opportunity to meet Shaquille O'Neal, all 7'1" of him. We were holding a benefit dinner for MRO and Feed the Children, and Shaq was one of our dignitaries in attendance. Even though my sports knowledge is limited (okay, nonexistent), I knew enough about him to realize just how cool it was to meet this living legend.

Having met Shaq, I may know a little bit *of* him, but I do not *know* him. There is no relationship. So I cannot, with any ease, introduce my friends to Shaq personally, much less speak personally of him to them, when I do not know him personally. It all hinges on relationship.

Similarly, we cannot testify to the gospel of God's grace if we are not experiencing it ourselves. I can tell others about God's goodness, but if I am not in relationship with God and experiencing His goodness firsthand, how can I testify to the true depth of God's grace? The only way God's grace and goodness can be personally experienced is through relationship.

In a romantic relationship, there are different phases that healthy couples walk through with each other that cultivate and strengthen their relationship. The cornerstone of any successful relationship is communication. You just cannot be in relationship with someone who you choose not to communicate with.

Our communication with God through prayer should be the cornerstone of our spiritual preparation. In Paul's first letter to the Thessalonians, he reminded them to pray continually (1 Thess. 5:17). In Paul's letter to the Ephesians, he painted a picture of preparation with his words about wearing the armor of God; he wrapped up his charge to be prepared by pressing them to continually and always pray (Eph. 6:10–17).

Are you unsure of where to even begin to pray? Try this:

Therefore, you should pray like this: Our ·
Father in heaven, Your name be honored as
holy. Your kingdom come. Your will be done on
earth as it is in heaven. Give us today our daily
bread. And forgive us our debts, as we also have
forgiven our debtors. And do not bring us into
temptation, but deliver us from the evil one.
For Yours is the kingdom and the power and the
glory forever. Amen. (Matt. 6:9–13)

Ask God to help you abandon your own ideals and
embrace His will and mission. Ask God to be your
source—physically, relationally, emotionally, and spiritually; He won't withhold the daily bread of provision.
Ask God to give you compassion for others and to help
you walk in forgiveness. Celebrate who God is; woo
Him with your praise. But whatever you do, talk to
Him, continually.

As the communication opens up in a relationship,
you want to learn more about the one you are convers-
ing with. In a romantic relationship, you begin to study
the one you love. You discover what he or she likes and
what he or she doesn't like. You become a student of
your love interest because you want to please that person. My wife has shared with me that when we were

dating, she memorized the entire field of NASCAR drivers and their numbers because she wanted to be on that level with me. Now *that* is love!

The more we talk to God, the more we should be drawn to learn about Him. Not out of responsibility, but because we want a relationship with Him. We should be drawn to His Word and desire to study Him and His character in-depth. Peter reminded us that we have to always be ready to share why our hope is in Christ (1 Pet. 3:15). We cannot possibly offer this defense if we have not experienced Him through both prayer and study.

Racing to win requires discipline, and we have to discipline ourselves to study God. Using the Bible, commentaries, and other resources, we should overindulge in discovering and understanding the biblical narrative. It takes discipline, but discipline makes champions.

Romantically, the more we learn about our love interest, the more we begin to adapt our lifestyles to please that person. As we discover through Scripture who God is, we should be transformed. The more we learn, the more our minds are renewed. The more our minds are renewed, the more we will be transformed. I believe this is at the heart of Paul's message to the Romans when he wrote, "Be transformed by the renewing of your mind, so that you may discern what is the

good, pleasing, and perfect will of God" (Rom. 12:2).
There is no greater testimony of God's grace than a life
transformed and in relationship with God.

Our preparation should not only happen in the
spiritual realm but in the physical realm too.

I remember being awakened one night by my phone
ringing at 2:00 a.m. As most guys would do, I ignored it.
My wife, on the other hand, was intrigued. Since it was
a local number, she urged me to call the number back.

"Spring Hill Police Department," the voice on the
other end answered.

"Yes, I just received a missed call from this number,"
I muttered half asleep.

"Yes, Mr. Froman, there is a police officer on your
driveway who would like to speak with you."

Let me tell you, there is really no good reason for
the police to be at your home at 2:00 a.m. My mind
began to race as I stammered around my bedroom
trying to get myself together and head outside. I was
certain that a family member had died, and I was trem-
bling as I dressed.

Once I made my way to the door and walked out
onto the driveway, the first phrase I heard from the
officer's mouth was, "Are you a chaplain?" Both relief
and a new wave of fear hit me as my mind reevaluated

what was happening. I began to assume I would now be called on to deliver dreadful news to one of our neighbors, in my pajamas, with crust in my eyes and morning breath.

As I answered, the officer handed me a state-issued ID and asked if I knew the individual. I did. It was someone I had been ministering to for a while, and I needed to speak for that person. At 2:00 a.m.

Mission does not always unfold how and when we want it to. It happens at all hours in all locations. Sometimes you may be called to serve someone in need when you are tired, fatigued, stressed, or overwhelmed. Other times you may be called to spend time away from your family. Occasionally you will have to invest your hard-earned resources in someone's life, and once in a while you may have to use vacation days to help meet a need.

In racing, not only does the race car have to be designed to go fast, it has to be designed to withstand the physical demands that will come its way. The car has to be built rigidly enough to withstand the grueling impact of racing five hundred miles at high speeds and in contact with forty-two other race cars. You can't win a race that you can't physically finish.

It is important to be physically and emotionally prepared to live on mission. The demands on time, relationships, and finances are very real. Preparing yourself and your family should be a priority.

As Jesus began His walk to His crucifixion, He called to the crowd, urging them that anyone who wanted to be His disciple should take up their cross and follow Him (Mark 8:34–38; Luke 9:23–25). In essence, Jesus was asking if we are willing to die to ourselves, to give it all up to follow Him. Are we physically prepared to follow Him?

Are we willing to follow Him if it means we could lose our job, our reputation, our stuff, or even our life? Can we race a good race if we can't work through serving the outcasts and the dangerous; if we can't handle time away from those we love or walk away from our comforts?

It may seem radical, but if we are not physically and spiritually prepared to respond in any of the extremes above, we are not going to win our race.

Racing is exhilarating and thrilling. Racing is also dangerous and exhausting. Without preparation we will have a hard time finishing the race, much less winning. We have to take time "at the shop" to prepare ourselves for what a life on mission looks like.

Chapter 2

Teams Win Races

Be in Community

"Your two, plus my two, equals five."

From Darrell Waltrip

Teamwork is the secret, if there is one, to the success of multicar teams in NASCAR. When you have teammates, you have a pool of information and resources that you can draw from. From set-ups and driving styles to suspensions and tire pressures, you find yourself with an abundance of information that single-car teams didn't have in the past.

If you are Dale Earnhardt Jr. and you are really hooked up, but Jeff Gordon is struggling to get up to speed, Jeff can come to you and look at all the data coming out of your team to see what he may be able to do differently to find some of your speed. If you stop running as well, but Jimmie Johnson keeps getting better, you can get with Jimmie's team and see what you can adjust to improve yourself.

I have a favorite saying when it comes to teamwork: "Your two, plus my two, equals five." On your own, if you have two and then you add two to it, you will always end up with four. It's simple math. But if you take your two, and combine it with someone else's two, then together you are always going to come out with more than you would have had on your own. That's because teamwork is one of the key ingredients of success.

One of my excuses for not being a more committed Christian in the early days of my faith was that, as racers, we always had to work on Sundays. The NASCAR schedule ran from February to November, so we were on the road week in and week out, traveling from city to city. Being that we were at racetracks every Sunday for nearly ten months out of the year, I couldn't have a "home church." I was a new believer, but I was missing the organized church community I needed to help grow. I didn't have a strong team alongside me.

Early on, there were some guys with good intentions who came into our sport and did some very positive things; they really brought the presence of the Lord to our community. However, one thing that was missing was the organized church atmosphere where you felt like you were at home on Sunday, in a church community with others.

In the late eighties, Lake and Rice Speed, Bobbie and Kim Hillin, and my wife, Stevie, and I started a Bible study together. We were trying to create that church community we so desired to be a part of. So it wasn't by chance that a gentleman named Max Helton introduced himself to us.

We met Max, who was living in California, during a race at Riverside International Raceway in 1987. Upon introduction, Max shared with us his heart. He told us that the Lord had called him to start a ministry in NASCAR. As exciting as that was, I had heard that story before. I'm a skeptic, so I asked Max, "So what did the Lord call you to do?"

"Well, He called me to move to Tampa," Max replied. "I'm going to move to Tampa and start a ministry in NASCAR." Max assumed that since NASCAR's headquarters was in Daytona, Tampa would put him close enough to the epicenter while utilizing some free office space he had been offered by a friend. Max didn't know the sport, so he didn't know any better.

I told Max, "If you want to be a minister in NASCAR, you have to move to Charlotte where all the race teams are." Max understood perfectly and he did just that—he left his church and packed up his family in California and moved them across the country to Charlotte.

We supported Max, believing he was just what we needed, but we were also concerned for him. He'd given up everything he had established in California and come to North Carolina with no money and no church. Max saw the need and gave everything he could to meet it. He was operating solely on faith.

Of everyone I've ever known who told me that God called them to do something, I know that the Lord called Max to do this. I know it because of the lasting impact he had. It was his vision, his determination, and his willingness to sacrifice everything that got Motor Racing Outreach (MRO) off the ground. From the day that Max arrived, he and MRO became an essential part of our sport. It had to be of the Lord, because a normal person wouldn't have been able to do all that he did.

Max and MRO brought a Christian community to NASCAR. We couldn't go it alone. Whether in competition or in ministry, if you are on an island all by yourself, you are only as good as you are. There is an old saying: "The rising tide raises all ships." In racing and in a Christian community, the more people you can bounce ideas off of and compare strategies with, the better off you will be.

That is the benefit of having teammates or being in community—being able to share information, feed off of each other, encourage each other, and grow.

From Kyle Froman

Growing up under the same roof as an extremely athletic father and brother, I always felt the need to prove myself athletically. They both shined at every sport they played—from baseball to football, soccer to swimming. The bar was set very high. Thankfully, I, too, had some sporting moments that were worth some highlight reels. One of my earliest shining moments came when I was around nine years old, playing Little League baseball for our community team.

As I stood at home plate, gripping my aluminum bat, I stared at the pitcher with sweat dripping down my back. I gave him one of those mean baseball stares—the one that says, "I'm about to knock this out of the park." The pitcher stared back, wound up, and released the ball. I shut my eyes and swung that shiny bat with all my might.

"Strike one!" the umpire yelled from behind the plate.

When I opened my eyes, I could see the dust settling around the pitcher's mound as he began to take his place again, glaring at me.

Our season was coming to a close, and that at-bat could potentially have been my last chance to prove myself that year. I attempted to reposition myself over home plate like I had been taught. I had two more pitches to make it happen, and I was determined.

There in the hot, summer sun, the pitcher wound up again and released the ball. I shut my eyes and swung. "Strike two!" the ump bellowed as the ball thumped into the catcher's glove.

My shoulders sagged as I opened my eyes again. My bat felt like a bag of bricks as I lifted it to my shoulders one more time, enduring this humiliation at the plate. Nevertheless, I pushed onward.

One last time I eyeballed the pitcher as he gestured to the catcher. He nodded and then hurled one last fastball toward home plate. I closed my eyes again and swung that aluminum stick with everything I had. Then I felt it—the unfamiliar vibrations of the bat connecting with the ball. I opened my eyes, scanning the outfield to see where it landed . . . and quickly realized that instead of driving the ball over the outfield fence like I had imagined, I had managed to clear the catch-fence behind me. Foul ball.

You would've thought I had just won the Little League World Series. After a year of swinging that bat time and time again, I had finally accomplished my yearlong goal. Earlier in the season, after several failed at-bats, my parents had promised that they would throw me a pizza party if I made contact during a game. Foul ball or not, all I had to do was touch the bat to the ball to prove myself, and I had done it! Pizza Hut never tasted so good.

As you would expect of anyone whose Little League career stats read "one foul ball," I was not the all-star athlete in school. I was accustomed to being in the bottom two anytime teams were picked in gym class for dodgeball, and I certainly didn't win any of our school's chin-up or sit-up contests. To be bluntly honest, I even failed to qualify for our school's jump-rope team and struck out in T-ball!

My lack of athleticism left me with a cynical, negative outlook toward teamwork. Within a team, I had nothing positive to contribute and my shortcomings were highlighted in comparison to other players. My negative self-perception when it came to sports, coupled with many benchwarming jokes, caused me to become jaded toward teams of any kind.

Personally, I'd rather run my race of life alone, without a team.

Maybe I was afraid of teams, or maybe I was too prideful to be part of a team. Alone, I didn't have to measure up to others, I didn't have to know as much as others, and I didn't have to be as good as others. Alone, I could be the hero, the shining star, and not get lost in the mix. Alone, I could stay in my comfort zone; I didn't have to stretch or grow. So it was my disdain for athletics and teamwork that drew me to racing.

My first introduction to motor sports came at a young age. On a sunny afternoon when other kids were out in their yards playing ball, I sat in the cool of our air-conditioned living room watching race cars whiz across the screen. Even though I had always been a "car guy," having exchanged rattles for Hot Wheels at a very early age, this was my first race to ever watch. I sat inches from the TV screen, my vision fixated as I watched the cars whirl around the track. The colors, the speeds, the sounds—they were all so compelling.

To a boy who had no athletic prowess, racing had everything going for it. There was no trying to connect a bat to the ball, there was no kicking with the laces of the shoe, there was no long pass down the field or three-point shots; it was just a man and his car competing for all the glory. Of course, at that age I didn't see the teamwork required to be competitive in NASCAR, nor did I understand the true athleticism of the competitors. All I saw was the Lone Ranger strapped into a really fast car, and all he had to do to succeed was drive faster than the other drivers.

It was while watching that NASCAR broadcast that I knew racing would be my thing.

Not long afterwards, during one of our regular family grocery shopping trips, I stood in the magazine aisle scanning covers while my mom faithfully traversed the store. In the middle of the shelf, one of the magazine covers stood out to me. On the cover of that September 1989 *Stock Car Racing* magazine was a bright orange Tide-sponsored race car, and the cover article title read "Waltrip's Hot." Fittingly, the purchase of that magazine led me to become a lifelong fan of Darrell Waltrip. In fact, one of my parents' favorite stories is telling about the first time I met DW. We were eating at one of our favorite Mexican restaurants—one that DW frequented, according to others in our community. I figured that if we ate there enough, we were bound to eventually see him. And one weekend, it happened.

As we walked into the door that evening, I scanned the restaurant as I normally did and spied DW and his first daughter sitting in a booth together near the door.

As a child, there are few things as epic as getting to meet your hero in person; it is the stuff dreams are made of. My mom didn't miss a beat; she grabbed me by the hand and we walked over to DW's table. My mom briefly introduced me as one of his biggest fans, and then DW spoke.

Frozen in a euphoric state, I couldn't reply. Quite literally, I lost the ability to speak. Nothing. An awkwardness quickly settled in, while I silently stared at my hero over the top of the basket of chips and bowl of salsa that separated us.

My mom, attempting to salvage the moment, dismissed us from their presence and walked me back to the waiting area, leaving me with a thousand things I wish I had said. As I sat with DW in his living room preparing to write this book, I couldn't help but chuckle to myself as I recalled this story in my mind. What a journey we all are on.

As I grew, I continued to lose myself in racing. While all the other kids in school were talking NFL, MLB, NBA, SEC, and more, I had my nose buried in the annual *NASCAR Preview and Press Guide*. This massive publication went everywhere I went—school, church, vacations, even my brother's ball games. Year in and year out, I memorized all the names, numbers, sponsors, manufacturers, tracks, and drivers' statistics in the publication. I quite literally became a walking NASCAR encyclopedia. It had become my sport, my passion, and my ambition.

The more I learned about NASCAR, the more I came to realize that individuals don't win races; teams win races. The reality is, alongside every winning driver is a team of men and women who are on board, working tirelessly and pursuing excellence together. It's the melting pot of talents and wisdom, experiences and gifts coming together that creates winning race teams.

I'll say it again: solo racers don't win races.

A winning race team is a great parallel to how Paul described the body of Christ to the early church in Corinth. They were a team coming together to function as one. Paul reminded them that the body consists of countless different parts—each one with its own special function, and each one equally important. Your legs need your feet to stand on, and your feet need your toes for balance. They all have to work together in order to take a step forward.

In racing, men and women come together with their own expertise, gifts, and talents. No one member of the team is any better than the other; they are all needed in their own unique way (1 Cor. 12:12–14).

This has always been an uncomfortable concept to me. Having constantly felt like the guy who would drag the team down, I perceived myself as dispensable. I couldn't find my place, and I never excelled because I was too concerned with being like everyone else on the team. I measured myself by everyone else, and when I didn't look the same, I believed I had nothing to contribute.

This occurred because I had the wrong perception of teams. Paul reminds us:

> Those parts of the body that we think to be less honorable, we clothe these things with greater honor, and our unpresentable parts have a better presentation. . . . God has put the body together, giving greater honor to the less honorable so that there would be no division. (1 Cor. 12:23–25)

We all have a place on the team, and even when we're convinced we serve an unimportant role, we should clothe ourselves with great honor. There is no room for any division within the body of Christ.

Not only do we all have a place on the team in the body of Christ, but we all need each other in order to run our own races with excellence. We cannot carry the burden of sharing the gospel of God's grace alone, nor were we designed to. We all have strengths, yet we all have weaknesses. We all have time, yet we all have limits. We all have energy, yet we all run out of steam. Together, we bring help and balance to each other.

Someone once said, "Teamwork divides the effort and multiplies the effect." In ministry, teamwork lightens the load you are carrying while strengthening the impact being had. This is a lesson that Moses was taught by his father-in-law, Jethro, about halfway through Exodus 18.

We enter into the story just after Jethro has brought Moses' sons and his wife, Zipporah, to where he was. We don't know exactly when or why Moses sent his wife and sons back to Jethro, but the family had just been reunited. No doubt it was a joyous occasion, but as with all special occasions, they eventually come to an end and reality sets in.

The day following the reunion, Moses had to get back to work, taking his place as a judge over the people of Israel. Undoubtedly, when an entire nation is journeying together, disputes will arise. This task of serving as Israel's judge was a sunup-till-sundown responsibility for Moses. Jethro took note and began to ask the tough questions.

"What is this thing you're doing for the people? Why are you alone sitting as judge, while all the people stand around you from morning until evening?" (Exod. 18:14). In other words, "Moses, why are you doing all the work while you have a bunch of people standing around?" Jethro, who was the priest of Midian, knew a little about leadership and delegation, and he saw the path that Moses was headed down.

Moses, completely missing the heart of what Jethro was asking, told him he was doing the work because the people came to him, and he would help them understand God's way. Moses was justifying the workaholic pattern he had settled into: the people needed him, and he alone was the one to meet their needs.

Jethro wasn't going to cut Moses any slack, and he quickly called him to task. "What you're doing is not good. . . . You will certainly wear out both yourself and these people who are with you, because the task is too heavy for you. You can't do it alone" (Exod. 18:17–18). Moses was setting himself up for burnout and putting the well-being of the people at risk. Something had to give.

What follows may be the earliest recorded leadership seminar in history. Following his painful projection, Jethro painted a picture of how Moses and a team of established leaders could reposture themselves into a healthier situation. Moses' responsibilities were too much for one man; he had to learn to serve as part of a team in order to stave off burnout.

Initially, Jethro affirmed that there were some things that were solely on Moses—things he could not pass off. It was Moses' responsibility to represent the people before God, and it was Moses' responsibility to continue to teach and instruct the people about the way to live. Moses had to recognize which responsibilities were his alone to fulfill before he could begin to delegate some of the tasks that were more generic in nature. Understanding what he had to do was the first step in realigning the system.

After Moses understood the tasks that he must fulfill, the next step was recognizing what responsibilities he could release. Jethro then continued with part two of his leadership seminar: Moses needed to select men to serve as commanders of thousands, hundreds, fifties, and tens. With this hierarchy they could judge the people. Important cases would still be brought to Moses, but all the minor cases could be judged by others. This delegation would ultimately lighten Moses' load, now that he was bearing it with a team of people.

Not just anyone could serve as a commander, however. Jethro emphasized the type of people Moses should be looking for. First, these men needed to have the cognitive ability to judge. In addition, they had to be God-fearing, trustworthy men. And last, as if Jethro had seen the future of politics, he said that they needed to be men who hated bribes.

Essentially, while Moses needed to lighten his load through shared delegation, he couldn't just pass his responsibilities to just anyone. He had to vet those he was going to give responsibility to, and those people needed to be held to a high standard. Without that standard, Moses' work would have been doubled rather than lightened because of the issues that would've been created.

In ministry, you will often find yourself in Moses' position. It isn't easy to take on all the work and carry the entire load on your shoulders. You can't do it. You will burn yourself out, and you will fail those around you. A person simply cannot serve others with any semblance of excellence if he or she is completely burnt out. So surround yourself with capable people—people who will help you carry the load, people who share your burden.

Not only do teams help protect us from the dangers of pride and burnout, but we know "plans fail when there is no counsel, but with many advisers they succeed" (Prov. 15:22). Everyone has their own stories to tell, their own experiences they've lived through, and the wisdom they've gained through it all. When we allow others into our circles, we can learn from them and grow from their successes. "As iron sharpens iron, so one person sharpens another" (Prov. 27:17 NIV).

I don't know it all, and I assume you don't either. I do not need to duplicate your mistakes, and you do not need to duplicate mine. But I do need to learn from you, because you have your own wisdom to share. So do I. As DW said, "Your two, plus my two, equals five." We need each other.

Don't be afraid to do ministry together.

Remember, even the Lone Ranger had Tonto.

Chapter 3
Running in Clean Air!
Be Guided

*"You're always fighting to get into clean air—
to get out front."*

From Darrell Waltrip

The impact of air on a moving car is called aerodynamics. When applied to a stock car while racing, the impact of air flowing properly over a car has a lot to do with how a car handles.

The aerodynamic effect has changed over the years as the engineering of stock cars has changed. Nowadays you want to get your car in front, in the "clean air." That's when your car makes maximum down force for the best possible handling and accelerating because the air can flow cleanly across the body of the car as it is designed.

When you're out front, you have all the air on the nose of the car, and if you notice the nose of these cars, they're always sloped, meaning that they're designed to skim right along the surface of the racetrack. In that position—when the car is riding just a few thousandths of an inch above the track—that's perfection! If the nose of the car touches the track, it messes the driver up. But just skimming along the surface, when you are creating the maximum amount of down force, that's when you go the fastest! Down force, as a result of clean air, is a driver's best friend.

So, you don't want to mess up your aerodynamics. You don't want to beat your car all up, knock your fenders in, and damage your car to the point where the air doesn't flow over it properly. You want to keep your car in good shape so that when you're in the clean air, you get the maximum down force.

That's why, as a driver, you're always fighting to get out front: that's where the clean air is. Now, as for the guy behind you, he's fighting a totally different battle. There is a void behind the lead car—what we call "the bubble"—and it is referred to as "dirty air." It takes all the down force off the nose of a car and produces what we call "aero push." Aero push is a nightmare! You're behind another car and you don't have any down force on the front of your car, so when you turn your wheels, your car "pushes" instead of being pushed down—it wants to go straight or not turn at all. The driver ahead of you is making maximum down force and running the fastest laps possible, and you're stuck behind him in "the bubble" because of all the dirty air.

Drivers will try to get a run and break out of the bubble to pass the leader, but it can be very difficult. It's just like getting your car stuck behind a big tractor-trailer as you're driving down the interstate. As you pull up to the back of that truck, you instantly feel your car start to bog down and waver a little, slowing down. This movement is the result of the dirty air the tractor-trailer is producing. You have to give it more gas to make the pass; only in racing, you can't give your car more gas. At the Daytona and Talladega tracks, you're already running wide open, going as fast as you can! So when you pull out and hit that wall of air—*whoop!*— you bog down and have no choice but to pull your car back in line.

This is when you have to be patient. You have to wait for the guy in front of you to make a mistake. Maybe he goes into the corner too hard and he pushes up enough that you get a shot to pass him down low.

But the guy in front of you has to make a mistake in order for you to get around him.

Clean air is a constant battle on the super speedway, particularly when you're running over two hundred miles per hour but also pretty much anytime you're running eighty or so miles per hour. The faster a car goes, the bigger the bubble the leaders create, and the more important clean air is. So you always, *always*, want to get out front!

You see this happen often on restarts after a caution. Drivers and cars that were running at the back of the pack decide not to pit, or maybe only take a couple of tires so they come out of the pit stops in front, gaining critical track position. When the green flag drops to restart the race, the race car that was running back in the pack now suddenly drives away and leaves everybody else behind!

In racing, there's nothing better than leading. You always want to be the leader. And you want to be out in the clean air. Nobody wants to run second; nobody wants to spend all their effort fighting dirty air.

Clean air is talked about all the time. These guys will tell you every day, "You know, if I can get this thing out in clean air, I can drive off and leave 'em!" You have a huge advantage when you're out front, in clean air.

From Billy Mauldin

The Daytona 500. It's the biggest race in NASCAR and the race that kicks off every season. Every driver who has ever sat behind the wheel of a stock car dreams of winning at Daytona! It is also one of the most unpredictable races of the season, due to the unique aspects of aerodynamics, down force, and clean air versus dirty air. This particular track demands that drivers pay attention to these elements. As Darrell Waltrip described, for the car running out front, it is smooth sailing when running in clean air.

Ministry is equally challenging. We have an enemy, Satan, who is constantly trying to destroy our faith, our hope, and rob us of the understanding that God loves us unconditionally. He does all he can to create "dirty air" and make our lives difficult and frustrating, hoping to ultimately see us crash. Like the driver at Daytona, we find ourselves often running in the "dirty air" he creates. By using lies and deceptions, Satan tries to daily throw us off balance or run us into the wall. He wants to see us crash, denying us our mission and purpose. He would like to see us give up on the race!

Jesus dealt with this directly at the front end of His public ministry (Matt. 4). Led by the Holy Spirit into the wilderness, Jesus was tempted three times by Satan, and each time Jesus responded with the Word of God, the Truth. Scripture tells us that after the third temptation, Satan departed and the angels of God came and ministered to Jesus. The truth of God's Word—and Jesus' trust in it—led to glorious victory. Truth is "clean air"!

While in college, I ran into a situation where I was struggling, caught up in circumstances where something was not quite right, but I couldn't put my finger on what was bothering me so much. For a few days I wrestled with the matter, and the more I thought about everything, the more I struggled to understand what was going on. Finally, while walking out of my apartment one afternoon, I caught myself saying out loud, "I need to know the truth!" I was tired of all the dirty air.

Right then and there, I was compelled to pray, knowing that the truth could set me free from the burden I carried. After a short while, my burden eased and I felt in my heart what I needed most: the confidence that God was in control. I broke out of Satan's dirty air and the "bubble" of confusion that he tried to create in my life. I was now back in clean air once again. God's peace in my heart was my assurance.

One of my favorite moments in all of Scripture is the hours Jesus spends with His disciples in the Upper Room the night prior to His crucifixion, as recorded in John chapters 13–16. In my reading of these passages, I see Jesus pouring everything He can into His closest friends in His closing hours with them. Reading now, it is obvious to us that Jesus knew what the coming hours would hold for Him: betrayal, beatings, crucifixion, and death. It is also clear that the disciples had no idea what was about to happen. In these final hours, Jesus modeled for them what it means to be a servant and taught them about the oneness that exists between Himself and the Father. He also assured these men that they would soon enjoy it as well. He poured into them, knowing that soon their faith would be shaken to the core and that "dirty air" was going to sweep over them.

In these sections of Scripture, I am drawn to the fact that Jesus loved His disciples so deeply. He had chosen them, and they were going to be the foundation of His future kingdom. Yet He realized they had no idea what was actually about to take place. They could not comprehend that He was going away. As they sat there listening to Him, they were clueless that God was about to change the world. Still, Jesus repeatedly taught them about running in clean air.

And I will ask the Father, and He will give you another Counselor to be with you forever. He is the Spirit of truth. The world is unable to receive Him because it doesn't see Him or know Him. But you do know Him, because He remains with you and will be in you. (John 14:16–17)

Truth is clean air! The truth sets us free!

As He was saying these things, many believed in Him. So Jesus said to the Jews who had believed Him, "If you continue in My word, you really are My disciples. You will know the truth, and the truth will set you free." (John 8:30–32)

Just like a car running out front, we are able to run our best race possible when we have truth in our lives. Truth brings clarity to our mission, our purpose,, and who we are in Christ. The Holy Spirit, the Spirit of Truth, guides us and directs as we run our race daily.

Four times in John chapters 13–16, Jesus teaches His disciples that He is sending them help: the Counselor— the Holy Spirit—who will be with them and in them to lead and guide them in truth. This is amazing for us as believers trying to navigate a fallen world full of lies and deceptions. We are called, and we desire, to live our lives with purpose and on mission, but at times we struggle to find our way. Why would Jesus repeat four times that the Holy Spirit would come for them unless it was of utmost importance that they understood this reality? Jesus knew that soon His disciples would clearly see and know their mission, and it would be the Holy Spirit who would guide them to this understanding. The Holy Spirit would sustain them when dirty air came at them!

Every day, each and every one of us encounters multiple lies and deceptions. God never intended for us to navigate them on our own. He knew since the fall of man that we would need help beyond ourselves and that He Himself would need to come and live within us to be our Teacher, Guide, and Counselor. We would become His earthly sanctuary.

> Don't you know that your body is a sanctuary of the Holy Spirit who is in you, whom you have from God? You are not your own, for you were bought at a price. Therefore glorify God in your body. (1 Cor. 6:19–20)

As God's earthly sanctuary, His true sanctuary, He fills us with His Holy Spirit to guide us every day in every aspect of our life. By His Holy Spirit we are able to know truth and combat Satan's lies in this world.

Often as chaplains our team will spend a great deal of time preparing chapel messages that we hope will be just the right word at the right time for those in attendance. We study and write, and rewrite and pray, and think through the message and rewrite again, trying to pull together exactly what we believe the Lord wants us to share. Finally, the time for chapel comes and we stand before a crowd and deliver our message. To the best of our ability we share our heart, close in prayer, and dismiss the audience. Before they have even risen from their seats, the lies start to flood our minds: "Boy, did I bomb!" "Nothing I said made any sense!" "I should have said it differently!" "Nobody is telling me what a great message it was; they didn't like it!" On and on the lies come at us like dirty air hitting a stock car running in last place!

At these times, you walk out of chapel and you just want to get away. Emotionally you get down—sometimes to the point you just wish the whole day were over! I have been there, wanting to disappear under a rock. It is in just such a moment that everyone needs a voice countering the lies and speaking to their heart. That voice is God's, and it is His gift of the Holy Spirit. As men and women desiring to have an impact on the world in which we live, we must grow in our ability to hear the voice of the Holy Spirit, which speaks only the truth into our lives. This is when we learn to stop and say as Jesus did to Peter:

> "Get behind Me, Satan! You are an offense to Me because you're not thinking about God's concerns, but man's." (Matt. 16:23)

Jesus recognized the deception and where it was coming from: Satan. To hear this must have startled and even confused His friend Peter; nonetheless, Jesus was not going to have His mission and purpose derailed by lies and deceptions. He was not going to get caught up in dirty air! We must be equally diligent and discerning in our daily opportunities to minister and serve. The Holy Spirit is present in our lives for just this purpose.

Interestingly enough, we can also experience dirty air and a "loss of down force" in our Christian walk from deceptions that appear very noble on the surface. One young man, shortly after coming to know Christ, was constantly told that he was going to be a youth minister—it was God's calling on his life. Wow! For a young man in his early twenties who had just been introduced to Christ, this was a big deal! Immediately he began to try and figure out how he would fulfill his destiny. When things did not seem to happen, and the opportunity to be a youth pastor never materialized, he began to question himself and even his worthiness to be in ministry. The comment came from good-hearted people proposing what they thought he would be good at because he was young and loved the Lord. Because it was a noble calling, spoken over him by trusted adults, he had all the more difficulty seeing it for what it was: a great idea . . . but not God's idea.

As time went on, the young man learned to follow the Lord's leading and voice on his own. He watched as God took him into areas and opportunities of ministry he never imagined. He heard the Holy Spirit for himself and came to understand what his mission and purpose was, both in the everyday small ways and in the long-term, as it related to his career. Over time the clean air of truth replaced the dirty air of a calling that was not of God.

The Holy Spirit's clean air of truth is ours if we want it. It is the promised blessing of God for all His children. It is our source of peace when everything else seems confusing, discouraging, or chaotic. The Holy Spirit gives us the "down force" we need to stay on track with our true mission in life. He helps us stay "out front," serving the One who saved us and who has now called us to share this good news with others.

Section 2

Receiving Your Mission

Chapter 4

Arriving at My Destination

Where Does God Want Me to Serve?

"I was only a fan then. I was racing at home, on a couple of dirt tracks. So I said, 'I need to get to Nashville,' because at the time, Nashville was a BIG deal."

From Darrell Waltrip

Life is full of stepping-stones. If you have a passion for something, you are blessed. All the time I ask young kids, "What do you want to do when you grow up?"

"I don't know."

"Well, what are you good at?"

"Aw . . . nothing."

So I ask, "What's your plan?"

Stevie, my wife, gets a little annoyed with me sometimes when I do this.

As I grew up I knew, and I had a target. I knew what my goal was. I had a passion for racing and was good at it. That's the other thing too; find something you're good at. Don't choose something and say, "Oh well, I'll figure it out." Maybe you're good at golf, or playing the piano, or maybe basketball. Whatever you're good at, do it because that's what's going to keep you going—when you know you're good at something.

That doesn't always mean every time you do it you're going to be successful at it. But when you know you're good at something and you have a passion for it, you keep going. That's how I was with racing. There was absolutely no reason for me to end up doing what I did other than, as a kid, I drove a go-kart and I fell in love with it. I was a natural at driving, and I knew I was good.

From that moment on, I told others that this is what I'm going to do with my life. They would ask me, "So, what're you going to do when you grow up?" And I would say, "I'm going to be a racecar driver." "Oh, yeah, right kid. How you gonna do that?" "I don't know, but I'm going to be a racecar driver!"

You have to have that passion, that motivation, that drive. Being content in your circumstances—being content in what you're doing—will make a huge difference in whether you succeed or not.

Now that I knew what I was good at and what I wanted to do, I had a game plan. As a driver I continued to get better. Owensboro, Kentucky, had two little racetracks, and I knew that if I could win each race there, I would be ready to go somewhere else, to move on. And, that's how I approached it. In Owensboro, I got to where I won every week and people hated me. So now I had to make a big decision, and I was on the fence about what to do.

Growing up, we lived on the Ohio River. Owensboro is on the Kentucky side of the river, and on the other side of the river is Indiana. One way was NASCAR and the other way was Indy car. I had a lot of my buddies at home who liked the open-wheel cars. I went to a lot of Sprint car races, Midgets, all kind of dirt track races in the Midwest. I went to a lot of races in Indiana, Illinois, and Ohio that featured open-wheel cars. But finally, I went to my first NASCAR stock car race in Nashville in 1965.

As I sat in the old wooden grandstands at the fair-grounds and watched the stock cars, I thought, *I love open wheel; it's really exciting. But I don't know, there's something about these stock cars. I really think I would . . . I think this is where I want to be.*

I was only a fan then. I was racing at home, only on a couple of dirt tracks. So I said, "I need to get to Nashville," because at the time, Nashville was a BIG deal. They had a big racetrack and two Cup races there every year. So, I figured, if I'm good, then this is the level I want to race at and this is the series, NASCAR Cup!

I remember Dick Hutcherson won the race. I'm sure Richard Petty was there, as well as Tom Pistone and Wendell Scott. I liked Nashville—I liked country music and the Grand Ole Opry, but most of all, I loved racing at the Fairgrounds. It was right down my alley! But, I didn't have a way to get from Owensboro to Nashville, and I didn't know anyone that lived there. This is how God's plan works.

A guy I knew named P. B. Crowell lived in Franklin, Tennessee. P. B. had some of the best race cars that money could buy—built by Bobby Allison. P. B. was a track champion at the Nashville Fairgrounds, and he liked to have fun. He would bring three of his cars to Owensboro and race with us at Whitesville on Sunday nights because they'd race in Nashville on Saturday night. He had three cars, numbers 47, 48, and 49, and they were in a league of their own. If you beat those guys, you'd accomplished something.

P. B. and I got to be really good friends. I was the only guy in Owensboro that could give him any competition. And, occasionally I could beat him. I had an old

'58 Ford. I'd run over him sometimes, knock him out of the way, and win.

In January of 1969, P. B. was testing a new car he had bought from Bobby, and while he was driving it, something broke in the car, flipping him several times. P. B. broke his back and was unable to race that year. Since he had two guys that drove for him, he called me one weekend and said, "I don't have anybody to drive my third car this week. How would you like to come down and drive it for me?"

"Oh, yeah!" I said. "Perfect!" And so . . . that's how I got to Nashville, and I won the race!

I'd run my course in Owensboro. I'd done all I could do there. P. B. also had a trucking company, so he called me up again and said, "How'd you feel about, you know, working for me? I'll give you a job. Work in the shop through the week and help with the trucks and then, you can drive the car on the weekend."

I got a job and I got a car to drive, all in one shot! Man, I jumped all over that. All I knew about was racing. The opportunity came to move to Franklin, Tennessee, right outside of Nashville, and I couldn't turn it down. That's how I ended up in Franklin and what was to be the beginning of my NASCAR career.

One step at a time, one place at a time, until I got to where I wanted to go.

From Billy Mauldin

On a beautiful spring day during my senior year of college at Appalachian State University, which is located in the mountains in Boone, North Carolina, I found myself in the student union where students would gather to catch up between their classes. Many of us had gotten to know each other through church, Bible studies, shared dorm rooms and apartments, or from just hanging out together. As I sat there that day, the primary topic of conversation was, "What am I going to do after college?" For many there was a great deal of anxiety about this unresolved issue. Although we were soon to have our diplomas in hand, the next step of life's journey had become a bit perplexing. Job opportunities were on the table for some; others were deciding whether or not to pursue a master's degree or seminary. And one of my friends was sincerely praying about what God would have him do regarding a couple of job opportunities presented to him. My friend's heart was set on serving the Lord, but he was struggling to discern what to do.

Just then, as we sat there, a lightbulb went off inside of me. I believe it was the Holy Spirit providing insight and wisdom—something that we all need and something that can only come from God. In that moment, I simply looked over at my friend and said, "Maybe we are all thinking and praying [worrying to some degree] about what we should do when maybe we need to be praying and seeking God for the place we should be." It was like a burden was lifted, at least for me. This was a different focus for prayer, and one I suddenly felt really good about. The job opportunities on the table for my friend were in different parts of the country. He also had the option to move back home with his family until he knew for sure what he wanted to do. Now his choice was thrown into an entirely new framework. As for myself, I found myself saying, "Lord, where is the place You want me to be?" I was looking at my mission totally differently!

This is the same situation described by Darrell Waltrip. Sitting in the grandstands in Nashville, he came to realize that Nashville was where he needed to be. He had gifts and talents. He could drive a race car. He knew one day he wanted to be a champion driver. He realized sitting there that the place for him was south, not north toward Indianapolis and open-wheel racing. Not really having a clue how it would all work out, he committed to heading south, and the rest is history.

The peace for me came in understanding that if I was where God wanted me to be, He would show me what to do. Do not worry about praying what to do; pray, "Lord, where is the place You would have me to be?"

Scripture came to my mind of men and women whom God had led, not to a task first but to a place. In each case, as they arrived where God wanted them to be, they then saw what He was calling them to do. I thought of Abraham being called to a land that God would show him . . .

> The LORD said to Abram: Go out from your land, your relatives, and your father's house to the land that I will show you. I will make you into a great nation, I will bless you, I will make your name great, and you will be a blessing. I will bless those who bless you, I will curse those who treat you with contempt, and all the peoples on earth will be blessed through you. (Gen. 12:1–3)

I was reminded of Moses being led back to Egypt so he could lead the people to a new land . . .

Then the LORD said, "I have observed the misery of My people in Egypt, and have heard them crying out because of their oppressors, and I know about their sufferings. I have come down to rescue them from the power of the Egyptians and to bring them from that land to a good and spacious land, a land flowing with milk and honey—the territory of the Canaanites, Hittites, Amorites, Perizzites, Hivites, and Jebusites. The Israelites' cry for help has come to Me, and I have also seen the way the Egyptians are oppressing them. Therefore, go. I am sending you to Pharaoh so that you may lead My people, the Israelites, out of Egypt." (Exod. 3:7–10)

I thought of Peter being led to the home of the centurion, where he himself would learn that God had given the gift of the Holy Spirit to the Gentiles as well as the Jews. . . .

While Peter was thinking about the vision, the Spirit told him, "Three men are here looking for you. Get up, go downstairs, and accompany them with no doubts at all, because I have sent them." (Acts 10:19–20)

In each of these situations, direction was given about a place these people should go, but not a lot of details about what they would specifically do. Once they arrived, God walked them through their mission step by step; but first, they needed to simply get to the place He wanted them to be.

Every year MRO conducts a training seminar. Men and women come from throughout the U.S. and Canada because they have a heart for ministry and, in most cases, at least some interest or involvement in motor sports. Many attend because they are curious about what MRO can share to help them be successful in motor sports ministry. There are also those who attend each year because they want to serve God but just do not know what to do.

Those men and women are all blessed with unique gifts and talents. They arrive with a heart to serve, and they are there because they are teachable. As we go through the weekend of training, we bring this issue to the table for them to consider: "Where is the place God is leading you to serve?" It is a different thought process than many of them have engaged in. Up until this point, their focus has been on "What do I do?" As they listen and think through it, you can see the Lord begin to speak to their hearts. In some cases this way of thinking helps them confirm that they are exactly in the place they need to be—at their local track or with the series they are presently serving. For others, you can see them begin to ponder a move to a new city or town—in some cases, even a new state. Some start out thinking the place for them is among a particular group of racers, such as stock cars, only to realize that God is moving them to a different place, such as motorcycles or powerboats. Their gifts and talents do not change, they just begin to discover that God will use them within whatever community He wants to place them.

I have sometimes failed to take the time to consider this question before making a decision and ultimately found myself in the wrong place. Shortly after college—despite the lightbulb moment I'd had in the student union—I got anxious because I had not found a job that I felt was fitting for a college graduate. I had turned one down a few months earlier because it was in a city that I didn't have peace about moving to. The work itself was something I was very familiar with and had done all through college. The company had contacted me because they knew I was a good employee and they wanted me on board.

As time passed, my anxiety grew, and one day I picked up the phone and called to see if I could still go to work for them. The job they'd offered me originally no longer existed, but they still wanted me, so they offered me another position. I accepted without hesitation and, may I add, without further prayer.

I moved three hundred and fifty miles to begin my career in a city where I knew no one. The job I accepted was nothing like what I had done before for that company. Three months into it I found myself struggling for joy, and peace and quickly came to realize that I had made a mistake. I had succumbed to the pressure to "do" something and had gone to a place where God had not called me. I realized that where I was before was where I was supposed to be: at home. So I called three of my buddies and told them to rent a U-Haul and get up there that weekend. I was heading home.

Upon my return, I settled back into waiting on God, and in no time at all I found a job that would write a new chapter in my life—a chapter where I would learn even more about what it means to truly wait on God. "Waiting" on Him is not a passive act; it is the exact opposite. I love this verse:

Those who wait for the LORD [who expect, look for, and hope in Him] shall change and renew their strength and power; they shall lift their wings and mount up [close to God] as eagles [mount up to the sun]; they shall run and not be weary, they shall walk and not faint or become tired. (Isa. 40:31 AMP)

When you look closely at the word "wait" in the original Hebrew, it means more than to "hope" or "expect"—which is what people usually think of. It also means "to collect" and "bind together." The act of waiting on the Lord involves us making every effort we can to draw near to Him and to grow in our relationship and intimacy with Him. We do this through prayer and by regularly reading and meditating on His Word. Our strength and ability to fulfill our mission begins with waiting on the Lord and allowing Him to guide and direct our steps.

God has a plan and purpose for all our lives. For the most part, we know that and believe it, but seeing it unfold can often be our biggest challenge. Waiting for Him to lead us step by step is hard when we live in a world that pushes us to get going and screams in our ears, "Make it happen! Successful people create their success!"

I am not implying that we should just sit on our hands and do nothing, but there is a step we can take that is important to fulfilling our mission. It is to first ask God, "Where is the place You would have me to be?" and then to live out our mission daily, open to the Holy Spirit. He may send us somewhere to accomplish His will even when we don't know all the answers regarding what we must do. This forces us to have a relationship with God built on trust—and that is exactly where He wants us. That is where He brought Abraham, Moses, and Peter, and it is the place He wants to bring us too. We should strive to be men and women who hear the Lord's voice and go where He sends us, knowing that He will provide whatever is needed to accomplish His will.

So what is your destination? Where is the place He is calling you to? It may be right where you are now, or maybe a whole new city, state, or country. Like Darrell Waltrip, hopefully we have all found something in life we are good at and enjoy doing. Hopefully we share a desire to be used by God to touch others' lives. We never need to question whether God wants to use us. The only question we may need to consider is, "Lord, where would You have me to go; where would You have me to be?"

As you ask this, I trust you will find yourself sitting in your own personal "wooden grandstands," where it will become clear to you that God has a "Nashville" just for you!

Chapter 5

When the Crew Chief Says Go

When Does God Want Me to Serve?

"When the boss says go, you go!"

From Darrell Waltrip

In 1986, our second race of the season was held at Richmond International Raceway (then known as Richmond Fairgrounds Raceway). The track had not yet been changed over to its current D-shaped configuration. Back then, it was a tight, slick half-mile track at the Virginia State Fairgrounds, surrounded by those red and white double-high guardrails that were typical of most of the short tracks we raced at. We had just come out of a third-place finish the week prior in the Daytona 500.

During our last pit stop of the day I had taken on four tires, and Dale Earnhardt had taken on only two. With ten laps to go, I was running second to Dale. I'd tried nearly everything to get around him, but I was still a little cautious of him. Dale was the kind of guy that if you hit him once, he'd hit you twice, so I wanted to try and get around him clean. We'd bump and I'd get inside of him, then he'd cut down on me and we would keep on racing.

With just a few laps to go, Junior Johnson, my racing team owner, came on the radio: "Durl, don't let that guy hold ya up."

I'd gotten inside of Dale twice, and twice he'd run me down into the grass on the inside. After my second bump, he'd made it clear with his hand signals that if I bumped him again, he'd send me spinning.

Junior had been watching this all from his place in the infield, and he came on the radio again: "Durl, I said pass him. NOW!"

Well, guess what? When the boss says go, you go!

Coming out of turn four, we headed down the front straightaway, taking the white flag. As we raced toward turn one of the final lap, I got into the corner as hard as I could. I was able to get into Dale just enough to nudge him up the track and get my race car to the inside. We were door-to-door through the corner, and coming out of turn two. I was able to edge just ahead.

As we raced into turn three on the back straight-away, I stuck to my inside line and started to pull ahead. I thought to myself, *Junior's gonna love this!* Just then, Dale turned left, hitting me square in the right rear with the front left fender of his car. His hit turned me to the right—and sent me head-on into that old fairgrounds guardrail . . . wide open! I didn't win the race that day. Neither did Dale, for that matter. Kyle Petty, who'd been running fourth, is the one who came around for the win.

Even though our team's day ended on the hook, we still finished in fifth place.

There were times over the years when I didn't want to listen to Junior, times that I'd argue the call he was making on the radio. Junior never liked that. He'd always come back at me and say, "Durl, do you want to drive the car, or do you want to run the pits?"

Most drivers learn to trust the guys running the pits, because they have all the information during the race. They can see the bigger picture, whereas the driver has a limited perspective from behind the wheel. If your guys say two tires, you take two tires. If they say four, then four it is. Whatever the call, the guys running the pits are in charge. And when they say it's time to go, that's when you go!

From Kyle Froman

With a decent-sized travel schedule every year, I try to optimize my time at home with my family. My bride, Michelle, and our two boys, Micah and Kaleb, always sacrifice a lot when I am away. It can never be said they are not a part of this ministry, because they give in unbelievable ways as a result of our following the call of Christ. Just ask them! Still, I never like missing the little moments of time with them, so the less I can be away from them, the better.

One of the practices I've put into play to maximize my time at home is to take early flights out of Nashville so that, whenever possible, I can get to the destination racetrack on the day of an event, as opposed to coming in a day early. This can usually be accomplished by catching my 5:30 a.m. connector to Atlanta and then jumping on to where I need to go from there.

While 5:30 a.m. does not sound all that bad to you cheerful morning people, I can assure you, it is not a joy to me. A typical 5:30 a.m. flight begins with the alarm (and two back-up alarms) blaring at me at 2:50 a.m. After about thirty minutes of stumbling and fumbling in the dark to finally make my way out of the house, I embark on a forty-five-minute drive to the airport.

On my way to the airport I always have a little chat with God. The words often feel the same, but my soul means what I'm saying: I ask Him to use me at the racetrack to share His truth and hope with people I come in contact with. I also ask that He directs me to people who need to hear His truth. By the time I am at the airport, I usually have just enough time to grow anxious while waiting on the shuttle bus, get frustrated waiting in the security line, and then rush down the terminal to my gate.

By the time I make it to the plane, any possible hint of morning sunshine has slowly dissipated and I am ready to sink into my seat, put on my earphones, and keep to myself for the short flight to Atlanta. I don't want to interact with anyone; I just want to "exist" for an hour.

If you travel a lot, you begin to learn how to keep to yourself on a flight and not look conversational. Earphones are fantastic, but stay away from the *Sky Mall* magazine; it just screams, "I'm bored and need someone to talk to!"

I remember on one particular flight a few years ago, I could tell that the gentleman sitting next to me had that look of "I am going to talk to you." I confess, I tried my hardest to look distracted. I checked the news on my phone while I waited for the cabin door to close, then I quickly shifted to my earphones. But once we had to discontinue the use of electronic devices for takeoff, I became a sitting duck.

Morning breath and all, I soon found myself engaged in conversation with a former worship leader who was really struggling with fulfilling his purpose in life. The hour went by very quickly as we found ourselves entrenched in conversation, and I believe God encouraged that young man through our conversation that day, helping him find some direction in his calling to serve Christ.

The rest of the day came and went, with me at the racetrack and nothing really notable happening. There were no major conversations, no deep spiritual issues tackled; it was just a "regular" day of presence at the track. As I traveled home following the race, I didn't feel discouraged; I just felt "eh."

The next Saturday I had another 5:30 a.m. flight scheduled. Same routine: wake up, fumble my way to the airport, ask God to use me at the racetrack, trudge through security, board the airplane, and look busy to stay out of conversation with those around me.

My attempts to look uninterested again failed as I found myself in conversation with a Canadian

NASCAR fan who knew very little about the Christian faith but who was curious about the interplay of faith and the NASCAR industry. Through our talk of racing and MRO's role within NASCAR, I was able to share the gospel message with him on that connecting flight to Atlanta.

Once I made it to the racetrack, it was the same story as the week before. There were no major conversations or interactions that stood out. It was a good day at the track with the community I was serving—a day of presence and relationship—but nothing more.

Week three. Alarm, car, prayer, security, boarding, and headphones.

My third consecutive 5:30 a.m. flight placed me in the seat next to a former Baptist serviceman who had converted to Buddhism, Southern drawl and all. I know there are some fantastic theologians out there, but at that time in the morning, I think all our blades may be a little duller. Regardless, he and I had quite the conversation about the dramatic differences between Buddhism and Christianity, what led to his conversion, and how he could again look to God in his life.

Week four . . . Are you beginning to see the pattern? On this fourth consecutive 5:30 a.m. Saturday, I found myself sitting next to a former Mormon who was now practicing Eastern mysticism and homosexuality. If you want to talk about having a tough conversation at that time of the morning (or at any time for that matter), try having a talk with that guy!

I continue to ask God to use me at the racetrack each time I'm on my way to the airport, because that is when I think God uses me best. Admittedly though, I can be a slow learner at times. These experiences are, however, teaching me another way that life is like racing: they're both all about timing.

In racing, it is easy for a driver to think he can call all the shots from the track. After all, he is the one behind the wheel with his feet on the pedals, so it's simple for him to assume he has complete control. The driver, however, is very restricted behind the wheel. He sees the immediacy of what he is doing, he feels how the car is handling, and he knows what is happening through the windshield and mirrors of his car, but he does not see the larger picture of the race that is unfolding around him. As a result, his decisions and timing can be off.

The team's crew chief, on the other hand, is in the ideal position to call all the shots. From atop his war wagon, he is able to see all the metrics for his team, monitor what is happening with other teams, look at race data, and monitor race progress to make the big decisions that will hopefully poise the team for victory.

Drivers have a narrow perspective; crew chiefs have a global perspective. Your perspective affects your ability to determine the best timing.

In our race in life, we can all too quickly find ourselves in the position of thinking we can call the shots from the driver's seat. Yes, we are the ones trudging through life, serving. Yet we put a lot of unnecessary weight on our shoulders when we begin to act as crew chief. We are prone to overlook opportunities because our limited perspective clouds our judgment.

On my early-morning stretch of flights, my timing was off. From the driver's seat, I was calling the shots, thinking it was up to me whether I talked to anyone or not. Because my life is being lived out on mission within the world of motor sports—which is where I have specifically asked God to use me—I was determining where I could best serve Him. Consequently, I focused solely on preparing for those moments at the track.

While it was a noble goal, I was wrong. I was dictating the timing of when God could use me to share my hope with others rather than following Peter's directive to be ready at all times to defend the faith and speak of the hope that we have (1 Pet. 3:15).

We know that it is God's desire that everyone would "come to the knowledge of the truth" (1 Tim. 2:4). This was affirmed in 2 Peter 3:9 when Peter shared that the Lord is not willing for anyone to perish but for all to come to repentance. It is God's heartbeat that everyone would enter into a relationship with Him. As much as I desire to see the community that I serve come to experience God, God wants *everyone*, regardless of where they are, to be in relationship with Him.

What's more, Paul reminded us that in order for people to believe in God, they have to first hear of Him. The only way they can hear of Him is by someone opening up and sharing Him. And the only way people are going to share about Him is if they are sent (Rom. 10:14–15).

We can't be sent if we aren't allowing God to call the race.

The immediate truth is that God wants all men to be drawn to Himself. So we have to be ready to serve and share truth at all times, with all people, in all situations, not just when dictated by the race we are personally running.

So does that mean we shouldn't seek a specific place of mission, that we should operate without direction? If God's desire is for all men to be saved, shouldn't our "mission" simply be every person we come in contact with?

Yes, and no.

In Luke, we see one of the experts of the law asking Jesus what he should do to inherit eternal life. Jesus answered his question with a question, asking him what the law said (Luke 10:25–26). The teacher answered, "Love the Lord your God with all your heart, with all your soul, with all your strength, and with all your mind; and your neighbor as yourself" (v. 27). Simply put, be so crazy in love with God that you put your everything in Him.

We all have passions—things that excite us. For some of us it is motor sports; for others it may be old cars or motorcycles. Some people are passionate about the arts and music, and some love computers and technology. We are all unique in the things that really fire us up. So when we begin to answer the question in Luke 10:25 for ourselves, we find that loving God with all our heart, soul, strength, and mind includes giving to Him our personal passions and desires to be used for His glory and purposes. If I am a computer nut, and I love God with all my heart, then I am giving God my passion for computers to use for His kingdom. I am saying, "Here is what I have. Please use it for Your glory."

I find myself serving in the middle of the world of motor sports through Motor Racing Outreach for that very reason. I took something that excited me personally—auto racing—and sat before God saying, "I give You everything, even my fundamental passion, to use for You." As I laid my passion before God, I saw the excitement of the on-track competition quickly fade and the thrill of serving people come to the forefront. My passion took on a new form as I laid it before God: my passion became people. That simple yet profound act of loving God with everything, including my passions, led me to MRO.

It is the direction of my mission to reach those involved in motor sports with the love of Christ. Having a focus like this brings quality, depth, direction, and relationship to ministry. But we cannot be so unilateral as we drive our race that we forget the big picture that our Crew Chief sees. He has the whole race in view, and it is His desire for *all* people to be saved. Sometimes His timing and directions are different than ours. We cannot get so focused behind the wheel that we forget to listen to His calls; otherwise, we could lose our race.

There are times I am at the racetrack to minister to the needs of a crewmember or a family member or a driver. There are times I am at the racetrack because God wants me to share with a passenger on a plane or a teller at a fast-food restaurant. From the car rental counter to the cashier at the store down the street, I've found myself having "church" with a lot of different people in a lot of different places . . . all as a result of being obedient and following God's lead.

Through the years I've had countless layovers in Atlanta, but amid all my delays, winded dashes, missed flights, and Occupy Delta sagas (that one is for you, Darren), there is one particular trip that really stands out in my memory. As one of my layovers was coming to an end and our plane was beginning to board, I noticed a young soldier, likely in his twenties, sitting just across from me.

The day before, I'd been struggling with the devotional I would share with our racing community over the weekend. As I sat in front of my computer, staring at a blank Word document, I would start typing—and then wipe out the entire document, only to begin typing again.

I struggled because I felt God leading me to teach on Creation. I was having a hard time because it is a very broad topic to cover in a short written devotional and a ten-minute chapel service. I fought it—staring at my blank document, writing and erasing for a good forty-five minutes. I didn't want to go there, but God wanted me to. I was wrestling God, knowing I couldn't win. And I didn't win. Ultimately, I surrendered to the Lord's leading.

So as I was sitting at my layover, I noticed in the hands of this young soldier the book *The Grand Design* by Stephen Hawking, an atheist attempting to explain Creation via physics instead of a Creator. It was obvious this young soldier was searching for meaning. I felt God leading me to do something. Our flight was boarding, and I knew I didn't have time to open up a conversation with him. At least, that was my excuse. But God continued to prod me.

As I got up to board, I knew I had to address God's leading. Then I remembered the devotional I had just written on Creation—the devotional I did not want to write. I walked over to the soldier and thanked him for his service to our nation. I then asked him a few quick questions about the book and why he had it. He shared with me that he had just started the book that day and was not very far into it.

I took just a few moments to share a very short form of my previous day's struggle to write the devotional about Creation. Then I pulled out a copy of it and left it with him so that he could have a glimpse of the truth of Creation . . . and of God's love for him—a love that put it in his hands.

I left to board my plane.

I never learned that young soldier's name, where he was from, or how he responded to the devotional . . . but I do know that God had a direct purpose for me in writing on Creation that weekend, and it was for that warrior. I pray that what God led me to write touches his spirit and puts him on a journey toward faith so that we can meet again in heaven.

We have to listen when God is talking to us, we have to move when He is directing us, and we have to be obedient when He is leading us, because we never know who He is using us to reach.

The timing of the race is not for me to decide. I am just keeping my hands on the wheel and my foot on the gas, following and responding to my Crew Chief, who is calling the race.

Chapter 6

The Ananias Effect

How Does God Want Me to Serve?

"I have no earthly idea why God said, 'DW, you are going to be good at driving race cars.' Nobody in my family ever had, and there was no reason to think I ever could. But somehow, some way, God said, 'You're going to be a racecar driver.'"

From Darrell Waltrip

I've had many people come to me over the years and tell me, "I want to be a racecar driver." I always respond with the same question, "Well, have you ever driven a race car before?"

"No, but I want to get into racing because I want to be a driver."

There is a lot more to being a racecar driver than just wanting to be one. Don't get me wrong—desire is an essential element of being successful at anything. Without desire, you will never be the best at what you do. You have to believe you can be the best if you really want to excel, but you also have to have the ability and be in the position to be the best. The same is true of any position within racing.

A team may interview someone who says they are the best tire changer ever seen, only to discover they are no good at changing tires at all. There are certain qualifications and qualities that go along with whatever job a person is hired to do on a race team. If you are a gasman, you have to be fairly strong and tall because the cans are heavy and you must be able to get that gas probe into the side of the car quickly and with authority. If you are a jackman, you have to have strength as well as great peripheral vision to see the tire changers on both ends of the car; you do not want to drop the jack too early, before they are done, and mess up the stop.

So the tall, strong individual who thinks they are a ringer at changing tires may actually be a perfect candidate to be a jackman or a gasman on the team. A person's size may not give them the agility they need to hop around the car changing tires, but it is perfect for other positions within the team. A lot of people come into racing thinking they are good at one thing, only to discover through the team's direction that they are gifted at something completely different.

Teams work when people are willing to do whatever is asked of them, even if it is something they feel unqualified to do. In fact, I'll fire someone who responds, "That's not my job; I don't know anything about that," when asked to do something that is outside the scope of their work. To be part of the team, you have to have a great mental attitude that says, "Here is what I want to do, but if you need me to do something else, I will give it everything I have." That is being a team player.

Growing up, my dad didn't drive race cars; he drove a Pepsi-Cola truck. In the summertime, when school was out, I'd ride around in that truck with him, helping him make his deliveries. On his route was a hardware store that Dad delivered to a couple times a week, and man, did I love going there! That hardware store sold go-karts, and I desperately wanted one of them for the Sunday races in the shopping center parking lot.

It took a little work to convince my dad that we needed that go-kart, but I eventually succeeded somehow and we got her home. The Waltrip family quickly became a racing family. On Sundays we would load that go-kart into the trunk of our family car and head off to church; afterwards, we'd take off to the shopping center to race. It was a family affair, and our whole family sacrificed a lot for me to do what I did. But racing came naturally to me, and I won nearly every go-kart race that I ran.

When I turned sixteen, I knew it was time to get into something a little bigger, so dad and I started to put together a '36 Chevy Coupe for us to run at the old dirt track—Ellis Speedway—in Newman, Kentucky. My first time out in that ugly brown car was a disaster. On my opening warm-up lap, I barreled down the front straightaway and completely missed the first turn. Once I got myself back on track and headed toward turn three, I found myself plowing head-on into the wall, ending my night. I didn't even make it one lap around that muddy track.

With practice, I eventually got a little better at dirt, but I still had moments of discouragement. Then, one of the two dirt tracks in Owensboro shut down, and when it reopened it was as a paved track. I was at home on that track; it was just like driving my old go-kart. Where the dirt guys were now struggling on pavement, I was excelling. My success on the pavement helped me land a deal driving for another team whose dirt driver wasn't cutting it on the pavement. They put me behind the wheel, and I haven't looked back since.

I have no earthly idea why God said, "DW, you are going to be good at driving race cars." Nobody in my family ever had, and there was no reason to think I ever could. But somehow, some way, God said, "You're going to be a racecar driver."

I was blessed to know what I was put here to do at twelve years old, and I was able to pursue that my whole life.

From Kyle Froman

One of my favorite people in the Bible is Ananias. Not the "I lied about withholding the money from the sale of my land and was struck dead" Ananias (Acts 5:1–5), but the other one, Ananias of Damascus.

We first meet Ananias at a very climactic point in Christian history.

In the opening of Acts 9, Saul of Tarsus is at the apex of his persecution of the followers of Jesus of Nazareth. Saul, a "Hebrew born of Hebrews" (Phil. 3:5)—a Pharisee persecuting the church—has been systematically destroying the church. Following the stoning death of Stephen, Saul's persecution of the church in Jerusalem is unleashed. House to house he has gone, dragging off those who were followers of Jesus and throwing them into prison (Acts 8:3). And now we see Saul on his way to Damascus.

That trek from Jerusalem to Damascus is about 135 miles and would have taken Saul and his entourage several days. The journey made a strong statement regarding Saul's commitment to persecuting the church. Saul carried along with him letters from the high priest, giving him the authority to take any followers of the Way back to Jerusalem as prisoners. It certainly wasn't going to be a cordial visit for the Christians in that region.

Along the way, something radical happened.

Around midday on their journey, as they neared Damascus, Saul had a life-altering experience. As he recounted this event to King Agrippa, he told of the bright light that enveloped him and his companions—a light that was brighter than the noontime sun. Then he was overcome by the voice of the Lord questioning Saul's persecution against Him.

Of course the officials traveling with Saul were shocked. They heard the sound, yet saw nothing. As Saul got up from the ground, he tried to open his eyes, only to realize that his vision had been lost. The group that was with him guided Saul into Damascus, per the Lord's orders. Saul waited there for three days. No food. No drink. Just waiting.

Parallel to Saul's encounter with the Lord, we meet the disciple named Ananias. Ananias, a resident of Damascus, was a "devout observer of the law and highly respected by all of the Jews living there" (Acts 22:12 NIV). When we are introduced to Ananias, we find him in a conversation with the Lord.

"Ananias, here is what you need to do. Get up and go to the street called Straight. When you get there, you'll find this guy named Saul, Saul of Tarsus. Saul is there praying, and I've shown him in a vision a man named Ananias coming to him."

The Lord's directive to Ananias was pretty simple. Go find Saul while he is praying, lay hands on him, and his sight will be restored. Simple enough. Or is it?

"Stop the train right there, Lord. I've heard about this guy named Saul. I've heard about the harm he's caused Your people all throughout Jerusalem. He's come here to do the same thing! He's got the letters in hand right now from the chief priests to arrest anyone who follows Your way. You know that, right, Lord?"

I think we all find ourselves in this position at one time or another. We hear God directing us to do something, and we begin to question Him.

God, don't You know who You are asking me to talk to? Don't You know that is my enemy?

God, You are asking me to go where? Don't You know that place is dangerous?

God, You are asking me to give up what? Don't You know that will make me uncomfortable?

That is the very position that Ananias found himself in. The Lord asked him to go lay his hands on one of the greatest persecutors of the church. The very man who had come to town to arrest men like Ananias was the man the Lord was now telling Ananias to go to. This was no Vacation Bible School task.

In his response, you can feel the fear and disdain that Ananias initially had for his mission. While he didn't say no, he questioned the Lord as if he had a greater understanding of who Saul was. It was known in the region why Saul was on his way there: the Christian community was surely in fear over his arrival. And now, Ananias had to go to him. He had to walk directly into the enemy's hands with no foreknowledge of the encounter Saul had just had.

The Lord replied, "Go!"

It really wasn't up for debate. The Lord had a task for Ananias, and all He needed from Ananias was obedience.

So Ananias went. He left where he was and headed to the house of Judas on Straight Street. When Ananias arrived, he went in to Saul and laid hands on him. Despite a fear of what might happen and the risk of coming alongside such a dangerous man, Ananias acted in obedience. He told Saul the Lord had sent him to restore his sight and fill him with the Holy Spirit.

Immediately something fell from Saul's eyes and his vision was restored. Saul didn't hesitate to get baptized. Then he spent time with the disciples in the region. Thus was the beginning of Saul's ministry.

Paul, formerly known as Saul, was arguably one of the greatest Christian thinkers and a leading figure in the advancement of the early church. He contributed nearly half of the New Testament via thirteen letters, and he inspired a great deal of Christian doctrine. From addressing domestic and social issues to matters of faith and salvation, Paul's contributions are many and great.

But when we look at Saul's conversion from Pharisee to Christian, there's no question: the story would not have unfolded as it did were it not for the obedience of Ananias to God's timing.

I know what you are thinking: Certainly God would not have let Saul's conversion—and the future of the Christian movement—rest upon one man's obedience.

Certainly God had a Plan B if Ananias didn't follow through.

Now we are getting to the heart of why Ananias is one of my favorite people in the Bible.

In Acts 9:12 is a part of the narrative that might be completely overlooked if we are reading quickly. The Lord said to Ananias: "In a vision [Saul] has seen a man named Ananias coming in and placing his hands on him."

Ananias was on the hook. The Lord had already given Saul a vision of Ananias coming to him. Saul knew who to expect—he had a name and a face! So there was only one person who could go to Saul, at that specific time, to complete the narrative. It wasn't Kyle, Billy, or Darrell. Anyone else would have nullified the words the Lord had spoken to Saul. Ananias had to go.

I imagine this wasn't the way Ananias had envisioned being used by God. I am sure that as he thought about how he could be used to encourage and exhort followers of the Way, tracking down and laying hands on a terrorist against the Christian church was not at the top of his list. This was dangerous and risky business, not the glorious, pedestal position in the spotlight. He definitely wasn't excited about how the Lord called him to act.

I think this often could be said of us when we have that conversation with God about how we plan to testify to the gospel of God's grace with our lives. We tend to dream of grandeur for ourselves—with the spotlight on us. We don't often dream of God using us in the difficult, dangerous, or risky situations. We don't dream of God using us as a supporting character. We dream of being the hero. Our ideals and God's purposes do not always align.

I first began to feel God leading me into motor sports ministry in 2002, as I sat at the Fairgrounds Speedway in Nashville one hot summer evening with a friend.

In the years preceding that moment, I had really developed a heart for ministry. I slid my passion for racing into the back seat as I began to pursue this newfound passion for ministry. I didn't really see how the two could mix and, at best, late nights at the racetrack seemed a distraction from the true ministry that happens inside the walls of the church (a supposition that is as far as the east is from the west). I wound up serving at a church under a dear friend and life mentor, and I really felt I had found my "place."

Then one weekend, a friend of mine called me up and asked if I wanted to head to the track with him to catch the races on a Saturday night. It had been awhile since I had been to the famed old speedway in the heart of the Tennessee State Fairgrounds, and every now and then, that back-seat passion liked to slide into the front seat for a trip down memory lane. I obliged, and to be honest, I was quite excited about visiting the track again. Sitting in those metal bleachers under the lighted overhang at that storied half-mile track always brought back many fond memories and childhood aspirations.

Watching the cars on the track that evening recalled the years I spent watching races there as a child. I vividly remembered the times I sat behind the painted red rails in the grandstands, dreaming about being a driver behind the wheel of one of those decaled race cars with the glowing tachometer and dash lights shining on the visor on my helmet. It was in those moments of recalling lost childhood dreams that I felt the presence of God right next to me in the grandstands. There—surrounded by thousands of other race fans, with cars circling the track in front of me—I had a very real conversation with God.

As I was feeling "sentimental" about my time at the track, God's voice began to penetrate my spirit. What He spoke to me was simple yet profound, scary yet exciting. "You are passionate about motor sports for a reason. Why don't you use it?"

As the presence of God continued to sit beside me, guiding my spirit, I made a very grave mistake: I stopped listening.

I didn't stop listening because I didn't want to hear what He was telling me; in fact, it was quite the opposite. I stopped listening because I was so excited about the prospects of what I was hearing. Right away, I began to interpret and plan for what I thought God was calling me to do instead of just listening when I was His audience.

My interpretation? That was easy—I was being called to be a racecar driver!

My grand aspiration involved having my own race car, and I would use it as a ministry tool to the racing community in Nashville. I had some really great ideas that I truly believed I could pull off. Meanwhile, I created my own dreams instead of pursuing God's purpose.

In pursuit of these manufactured dreams, I did what any prudent, engaged college student working for minimum wage would do: I went online and bought a race car using a high-interest credit card, sight unseen.

Yes, a credit card. I am almost certain I can hear the Dave Ramsey faithful grunting as I type this.

As spontaneous as that sounds, I did at least have a plan. Prior to the purchase, I had shared my vision with a local radio station that was going to partner with me in the endeavor, eliminating the financial burden. After several meetings, the station's sales team had come on board, offering to sell sponsorships for me, underwriting the cost so that their call letters could be displayed on the door. To me, it was a great confirmation that I was on the right track.

The day after I took delivery of a used Legends International race car direct from Oklahoma, I scrambled to get the car's measurements to a nearby graphic design shop so I would be ready for the "big reveal" that evening with the radio station at a local concert. It was definitely a last-minute scenario since we did not even have a trailer yet! While I went one direction to work on the graphics with my mom, my dad went the other to hunt down a U-Haul trailer to get the car to the unveiling. Somehow, all of the pieces came together and we made it!

Days after the grand reveal, that partnering radio station pulled out of the deal. After a few days of radio silence (pun intended), I reached out to the radio station to see when we could move forward with our sponsorship plan. The reply? They had discussed it, and it wasn't something they felt they wanted to pursue any longer. I was left with a worn-out race car, a pile of debt, and a broken dream.

I let the race car sit in my parents' garage for several months while I attempted to wrap my mind around what to do. After countless failed attempts to secure a new financial backer, I had to put a For Sale sign on my broken dream.

Initially, I was contacted by a very successful country music songwriter who writes for some of the biggest names in the industry. I was optimistic. Through our conversations, we settled on a partial cash trade that would at least eliminate half of the debt I owed and leave me with a racing go-kart that I could sell for the remaining balance of my debt. At this point, half was better than nothing; at least I still had something I could work with.

The sale of the go-kart didn't prove to be as easy.

Not long after listing all the details of the kart online, I received an international phone call while sitting at my favorite Mexican restaurant with my then pastor, Jason. Answering the phone, I quickly picked up on a thick Nigerian accent on the other end of the line.

After a quick exchange of pleasantries he began to ask me a long list of questions about the kart I was selling. From the condition of the frame and bodywork to the mechanics of the engine and how many races the kart had on it, this man knew his karts.

Through that conversation and subsequent ones, he shared with me that his son was an aspiring racer in Nigeria, and that quality American-made karts were hard to come by. Along with my kart, he would be purchasing three other karts stateside and having them crate-shipped to Lagos, Nigeria (don't get ahead of me). In order to do so, he needed someone to pay the shipper stateside upon pickup of my kart. To facilitate the payment, he would send me a cashier's check for double the amount of my kart so I could use the extra money as a payment to the shipping company.

The check arrived. The bank cashed it. The journey had ended. Or had it?

There was no aspiring young Nigerian racer waiting on an American kart. There was no shipping company. In fact, the excess money that I wired to the supposed shipper went straight back to the fraudster's pocket— and he disappeared as quickly as he entered the conversation. And now I found myself with a sizable debt to my bank for passing a fraudulent check.

What began as an invitation from God to pursue ministry ended with a broken dream and a wild road that included a fraudster living in Lagos, Nigeria, a counterfeit check, and a whole lot of heartache. Did I mention I was in college, engaged, and working for minimum wage?

What started as an awesome vision for a way to reach people for Christ in a unique and exciting way ended with me on the fringe of giving up ministry altogether. I was overwhelmed, frustrated, angry, and heartbroken.

It was when I was at the bottom that I realized I never even bothered to ask God how He wanted me to serve. I had missed it.

When the Lord spoke to Ananias, directing him to "go to the street called Straight" (Acts 9:11), Ananias would have quickly recognized the street: it was the main east-west thoroughfare through Damascus. In Roman times, covered porticos with local shops in them lined the street alongside a mix of homes. It was a familiar, busy area.

When the Lord told Ananias to go there, he could have cut the Lord off, making the decision on his own as to what he wanted to do when he got there. He could have dreamed of testifying of the gospel to travelers on the busy thoroughfare, being a beacon of light and hope to the desperate people of Damascus. He could have missed the object of the Lord's direction by not continuing to listen, missing a moment of impact in Saul's life that ultimately reshaped the course of Christian history.

But cutting the Lord off is exactly what I did. I listened to where God wanted me to go, but I didn't ask how He wanted me to serve there. I took the map, without the destination marked, and I ran with it. And now, at my point of brokenness and desperation, I was realizing I didn't wait for God to finish speaking to me.

When I hit bottom, I was ready to listen.

When I surrendered and listened to God, the course of my situation began to transform. Through a series of different relationships and experiences, God led me to be introduced to Motor Racing Outreach and their methods of doing life with the racing community, testifying about the gospel of God's grace through chaplaincy and connection.

I began to see the beauty of serving that way. It was something I could never have imagined when I first began to hear God speaking to me. It was a wonderful paradigm where my desires were no longer the focal point (as they would have been if I had a race car);

instead, the relationships and the community became forefront. In essence, I would disappear behind the scenes into a beautiful world of serving others right where they were so that they could experience God.

Ananias never became a "heroic," recurring figure in the Bible. In fact, after his encounter with Saul, we don't hear about him again other than Paul's brief recounting of him in Acts 22. While playing a seeming support role in Paul's conversion story, everything hinged on his obedience. He answered his call to serve regardless of the danger associated with it, and the lack of "fame" he would draw from it. It wasn't an apparently grand call to speak to thousands of people but rather, a request to obediently serve just one.

When we grasp that concept, we begin to understand what Paul was writing about in Romans 12:1:

> Therefore, brothers, by the mercies of God, I urge you to present your bodies as a living sacrifice, holy and pleasing to God; this is your spiritual worship.

As Paul continues, he reminds us to not be conformed to the world or influenced by what it has to offer. We cannot afford to be shaped by stardom and fame, money and power. The things that the world places priority on cannot be where our priorities fall. Instead, we have to renew our minds so that we know what the good, pleasing, and perfect will of God is.

God tells His followers to go. Of that there is no doubt. Still, we need to be obedient as we go, making sure our destination is mapped by Him, and not us.

Chapter 7

The Invited Guest

*Why Does God Want
Me to Serve?*

*"The short version: it doesn't pay to be loud,
arrogant, and obnoxious!"*

From Darrell Waltrip

In 1973, I was a rookie and I was a hotshot. I mean, I was coming into racing with a lot of fanfare. I'd run a lot of what was then called Late Model Sportsman's races.

In '72, I ran five Cup races and finished in the top three twice, finished sixth in Charlotte, and led Talladega. So, I was pretty cocky coming in. In '73, my first full year as a rookie candidate, I was pretty outspoken, opinionated, and I had my own ideas about how things should be done.

In Atlanta that year, qualifying got rained out. Even though I was a rookie, I had a fast car and I'd been fast in practice, but when the rains came, NASCAR decided they would set the field by points. Well, I was eighteenth in the points at that time. We'd only had two or three races. I didn't go to Riverside—the very first race—because I didn't have any road course experience and didn't have the money to go out west. But I finished pretty good at Daytona and wherever else we'd been to that point.

Because I was eighteenth in the points, I figured I'd start eighteen when they announced they were going to set the field by points. Well, NASCAR decided they would start the first seventeen cars by points and everybody else would have to draw out of the Bingo Ball. Now, why would they pick seventeen? Why not choose the top ten, top fifteen, or top twenty? How did they come up with seventeen?

Anyway, I decided, "It doesn't matter; I'll take my chances." So I went and drew a Bingo Ball . . . and I drew dead last! Now I was not only *not* starting eighteenth but starting dead last among forty-two!

That really ticked me off. Needing answers, I went out after we drew and found a NASCAR official. "Who's in charge of this deal anyway?" I asked.

"That would be Lin Kuchler," he said.

"Well, where is this Lin Kuchler guy?"

He said, "He's having a press conference down at the media center. It's right at the bottom of the hill there."

When I walked into the pressroom, the media was there and Cooper was explaining why they had chosen the top seventeen, forcing everybody else to draw out. Then he said, "Any questions?"

And I said (and the media guys are all there), "Yes, sir, I have a question!"

"Oh, really? And what's your question there, Mr. Waltrip?"

"Maybe these guys in here already know, but I don't. Why did you choose the top seventeen? I mean, I'm eighteenth. Why didn't you say top eighteen, top twenty?"

I was taking over the press conference.

"If you'll just calm down a minute," he said, "I'll explain it to you. There are seventeen guys who have run all the races. You didn't go to California. You missed one race, so we took the top seventeen who had run them all. They start by points."

I said, "Well, that's the dumbest thing I've ever heard of. What difference does that make? I'm eighteen in the points . . . what difference does it make that I went to Riverside or not?"

Lin responded, "Well, that's just how we do things."

I said, "Well, I think it's a really dumb way to do something."

The entire time, the media was eating this up. Then Lin Kuchler got embarrassed because I was going a little overboard.

I was really mad. I had a really fast car, and I didn't want to start dead last. And to add even more insult to the injury, a rookie who had never raced in Atlanta, never raced anywhere, drew the eighteen!

That was the beginning of my rookie year, and for the rest of the year, I was an antagonist. Lennie Pond was also a rookie that year. He's from Virginia, and he was a nice man—really calm, easygoing. If you told Lennie, "Park your car in the garage; you aren't racing this weekend," he'd say, "Okay. That's fine. No problem." Me, on the other hand, you'd have a fight on your hands.

At the end of the year I was highest in the points, I had the best finishes, and I'd made the most money. I had all the numbers in my favor. But NASCAR arbitrarily decided who would be Rookie of the Year. And guess who was selected? Lennie Pond.

That should have taught me a lesson, but it really didn't. It just aggravated me that much more. And that really "bit" me for a long time.

I don't always agree with NASCAR's decisions, and I got off on the wrong foot as a rookie. But that was the difference between Lennie Pond and me. Lennie was humble. He was gracious. And in the end, Lennie got the recognition as a driver and for how he handled himself. The short version: It doesn't pay to be loud, arrogant, and obnoxious!

From Billy Mauldin

I remember the first race I ever attended as a chaplain with Motor Racing Outreach. My wife, Julie, and I flew out to Evansville, Indiana, for what was at that time a race with the H1 Unlimited Hydroplane Series. Some of the most spectacular racing I have ever seen is hydroplane racing. For those not familiar with this form of racing, these are thirty-foot boats that average around 6,800 pounds and are powered by turbine engines. They are capable of running over two hundred miles per hour and are the fastest boats on earth!

Julie and I went to Evansville not knowing a single person involved in this racing series. For that matter, we didn't know a single person in Evansville! We were given instructions to meet a gentleman at the race site who would provide us with credentials for the weekend. Excited and a bit naïve, we boarded a plane and headed off, looking forward to serving as the first-ever chaplains to the Unlimited Hydroplane Series!

We arrived and checked into our hotel and then headed down to the pit area along the Ohio River in downtown Evansville to meet with our host. "Thunder on the Ohio" was the name of the event. After a little time and effort, we found our host, acquired our credentials, and began our weekend.

As newbies to this type of ministry, we quickly realized that it was going to take time to build relationships. We knew no one, and no one knew us. Word spread that we were there, and a few people said hello, but for the most part we were on our own, wandering the pits, just trying to figure everything out. Needless to say, the first weekend was a bit uneventful. We learned a lot about this less familiar form of racing just by watching, but I must admit, we left wondering whether this was really going to be worth the time and effort.

My thought coming into the weekend was that the people would be more excited to see us. I mean, we were chaplains with MRO, the series that serves NASCAR! I felt they were pretty fortunate to have us there for them! They'd never had a chaplain before, and here we were!

In no way were we anything but courteous, polite, and grateful for the opportunity to be with these people, but where was all the excitement at having us among them, serving and caring for them? After that first weekend in Evansville, neither Julie nor I was sure where this was all going to lead.

Whoever exalts himself will be humbled,
and whoever humbles himself will be exalted.
(Matt. 23:12)

A few weeks later we found ourselves at our second event—again on the Ohio River, but this time in Madison, Indiana. Upon arriving in the pit area, we began what had become our routine the week before: just wandering around, smiling, trying to be friendly and open to conversation. After being there for a couple of hours, one of the race directors came up to me and introduced himself. I thought, *Now we are getting somewhere!*

He explained to me that they were glad to have us there and they looked forward to us being with them for the season. He also shared with me that he planned to introduce me in the drivers' meeting (they call them pilots) later that day and he wanted me to make sure I was on hand and up front. And to top it off, he wanted me to close in prayer!

God is on the move now! I thought to myself. *The big moment has come where I will be formally introduced and close their meeting in prayer, just like we do in NASCAR!*

At the meeting the race director covered all the typical information and recognized a number of special guests. Last but not least was their special guest—me— their chaplain who would now be traveling with the series. After the director introduced me, he informed the group that I would be closing the meeting in prayer and asked if anyone had any questions for me. I was sure someone would want to know more about all we did in NASCAR, or maybe just want to express how thankful they were to have me there with them. This was finally the moment when the importance of my presence was going to be recognized and the community would see as a whole how blessed they were!

Well, not a hand went up, but from the middle of the group, a question was shouted out: "Can you do exorcisms?" The group busted out laughing, and the race director looked at me and I looked at him. *Oh boy,* I thought, *I can see I am being taken really seriously!*

Now I truly thank God that at this moment He gave me the wisdom I needed. And even though I wanted to be seen and respected as their chaplain, I did have enough sense to know that it was going to take time to earn their respect and trust. With only a brief moment of pause, I responded, "If you can hold them down!" *Again, thank You, Lord, for Your peace and calm in what was a tense moment for me.*

The group once again burst out in laughter and the gentleman who asked the question gave me that smile that told me I had earned his respect in that moment. I then closed the meeting with prayer.

As the season went on, Julie and I traveled with the community and, over time, we got to know many more of the people who were part of the series. It took time, but as they came to know us, and we came to know them, we developed a few really nice friendships. When the season ended with a race on Pearl Harbor in Honolulu, Hawaii, we left truly feeling like we had become a part of the community, trusted and respected. What started out as a bumpy journey ended smoothly due to a simple principle we always kept in mind. It is one Max Helton, the founder of MRO, had taught me: "Always remember, you are the invited guest!"

What a great truth for us all to remember. We can easily develop a mentality that as men and women of God, the world needs us and we are thus entitled to their openness and respect. Indeed, the world does need us—or more accurately, the Jesus we have to offer them—but most of the time it takes a while for them to realize it. Until then, we must be careful not to impose on them. As the "invited guest" mentality governs our behavior, we will avoid some of the pitfalls that come with imposing ourselves on others. The world will, in turn, see us as people who sincerely appreciate them and the opportunity we have to be a part of their lives.

This means setting aside our personal agendas and seeking what we can do to help those whose lives we have the wonderful opportunity to be a part of. It means we get rid of any sense of entitlement we think is ours due to our background, position, or associations, and we seek one thing only: what is best for those we have the opportunity to care for. Jesus modeled this for the disciples at the Last Supper when He rose up from the table and washed the disciples' feet.

> When Jesus had washed their feet and put on His robe, He reclined again and said to them, "Do you know what I have done for you? You call Me Teacher and Lord. This is well said, for I am. So if I, your Lord and Teacher, have washed your feet, you also ought to wash one another's feet. For I have given you an example that you also should do just as I have done for you." (John 13:12–15)

The disciples needed to learn that God looks at everything differently than we do. He is looking for the humble heart that is willing to serve and be dependent on Him. For the most part though, we believe and act the exact opposite. We pridefully believe that we deserve to be served and have no need of anyone. In fact, we take great pride in our ability to handle things ourselves, without help from anyone. This is not just the way of those who do not know God. It also creeps into the church and church leadership. We must always guard our hearts to remain humble men and women who are willing to wash others' feet.

> He leads the humble in what is right and teaches them His way. (Ps. 25:9)

Humility is instrumental in longevity and covers a multitude of mistakes. Every year a new group of rookies makes it into NASCAR. They compete for the title of Rookie of the Year, and like most of their counterparts in any sport, they are under a bit of a microscope, with everyone watching to see if they really have what it takes to make it.

Most every driver that ever gets the chance to drive in NASCAR's premiere series—the Sprint Cup— has been a champion at some level. They gained the attention of team owners and sponsors because they are winners. However, when they get to the Sprint Cup series, it is a whole new deal. Now they are racing against an entire field of drivers who are all past champions in their own right.

The competition is at the highest level possible and, for the rookie, it is at once exciting and pressure-filled. There is a lot to learn and new relationships to be made. As a rookie, you are learning every race and mistakes are made. Seldom intended, but mistakes nonetheless, and how a rookie handles these moments can go a long way in determining his or her future in the sport. Rookies who are mindful that this incredible opportunity has been given to them, and who conduct themselves with this mind-set, find themselves more quickly forgiven for mistakes. They find they are extended advice, encouragement, and coaching from others in the sport who had to travel the same road of experience themselves.

A person's pride will humble him, but a humble spirit will gain honor. (Prov. 29:23)

Drivers who act as though they have it all figured out and are in no need of help soon struggle to find the "friends" every driver needs on the track to be successful. Their longevity becomes questionable and their mistakes are not soon forgotten.

As it is on the track, so it is in ministry. A little humility and recognition that we need help in accomplishing our mission will serve us well in finishing our race!

When drivers do win, they have the moment they all dream of: a trip to victory lane! It is in victory lane that they are the center of attention and the hero of the day. Everyone wants to talk to them and the cameras are focused on them. Upon climbing out of the car, what do winners most often say? *Thank you!* The wise winners thank their team, their sponsors, their family, the fans, and anyone and anything else they can think of! Giving thanks—genuine thanks—is the sign of a champion. It is the sign of a team player.

There are also those who finish the race but did not win. When they are spoken with after the race, they too recognize that the opportunity they just had was not something they could have done without the help of others. NASCAR and its drivers are known for their relationship with their teammates—the fans and sponsors—and these same drivers, although maybe disappointed and frustrated, still take the time to express their thanks to those who made the day possible.

Now we ask you, brothers, to give recognition to those who labor among you and lead you in the Lord and admonish you, and to regard them very highly in love because of their work. Be at peace among yourselves. And we exhort you, brothers: warn those who are irresponsible, comfort the discouraged, help the weak, be patient with everyone. See to it that no one repays evil for evil to anyone, but always pursue what is good for one another and for all. Rejoice always! Pray constantly. Give thanks in everything, for this is God's will for you in Christ Jesus. (1 Thess. 5:12–18)

As men and women living our lives with purpose and on mission, we do well to always walk humbly and remain mindful that we cannot do it on our own. Those who allow us to be a part of their lives have given us a gift, and we are wise to act as "invited guests," giving recognition to those who help us along the way.

It takes a team to win, and seldom do lone rangers accomplish as much as two, three, or more committed people working together. Working together, let's give thanks in all situations, realizing that we have already won the race because we are alive in Christ Jesus our Lord!

Section 3

Living on Mission

Chapter 8

Friends in the Pits

Live in Relationship

"When you put on that helmet and strap into that car, you become a gladiator."

From Darrell Waltrip

Gladiators do battle. When you put on that helmet and strap into that car, you become a gladiator. I remember one race in particular—a fall race at Rockingham—when Ricky Craven and I were battling each other hard inside the top ten.

We'd been fighting for position for the better part of the day. For the most part I had been beating him, but he continued to tag right along behind me. We both had something to prove as we raced into the final lap. Through turns one and two, I maintained my lead. On turn three Ricky dive-bombed his car into the corner without even lifting and body-slammed me right into the fence. I wrecked my car, and Ricky went on to finish the race.

I was livid. I was still recovering from a broken leg after a previous wreck, and I had just taken another hard lick against the wall. I sat up on the track while the cars that had finished the race made their cooldown laps and lined up to enter the garage. Once I managed to get myself out of my wrecked car, I ran down the track toward where Ricky was parked. I still had some pain in my leg as I limped. I must have looked like Chester from *Gunsmoke*.

By the time I finally managed to stumble across the track, Ricky drove for the garage . . . and that really made me mad! So I kept chasing him, and I chased him all the way into the garage. When I finally got to where his car was parked, I jerked down his window net and said, "I want you to sit right here a minute, because when I catch my breath, I am gonna whoop you!"

My crew was quick to jump in and pull me away from Ricky's car, corralling me back into my hauler. They got me up into the driver's lounge at the front of the hauler, but I was still hot. "I'm gonna get my uniform off, get my clothes on, and go over there and teach that boy a lesson!"

In the middle of my fussing, here comes Max Helton. Max was our Motor Racing Outreach chaplain at the time. He knew that I was upset and came into the driver's lounge to try and speak some sense into me. When he made it up to the front, he closed the door and did not hesitate to let me know I was making a fool of myself. He urged me to calm down and reminded me of the example I was setting for other drivers in the community. He knew this wasn't who I was, and he didn't want me to do something I'd regret.

I wasn't calming down.

Finally, Max threw his arms across the door to block me in and said, "If it makes you feel any better, beat me up! That way you won't go out there and make a fool of yourself. Give me as much as you want!"

Of course, when he started in with that, I looked at him, and he looked at me, and we both just started laughing. I realized how ridiculous I was being, and that calmed me down.

The next week Max asked me if I was going to be at chapel. I told him I had an appearance to make and really wasn't planning on it. Max said, "I really need you to come to chapel to pray. My brother was supposed to and couldn't make it, and I need you to open us in prayer." I told him I'd be happy to.

In chapel, Stevie and I sat on the front row so I could pray and then leave for my appearance. Since she and I were sitting on the front row, we couldn't see anything going on behind us until I stood up to pray. It was then, as I looked across the room, that I saw Ricky sitting right behind where I was sitting.

I looked at his face and I could tell what he was thinking. *This guy is gonna pray for us? This guy who was going to kill me last week is gonna say the prayer?* I stood there a moment, looked at him, thought about it, and said, "Folks, I have something I have to confess. I'd like Ricky Craven to come up here."

At first he just looked at me and was probably thinking, *Waltrip's gonna whoop me in front of this whole church crowd.* And though Ricky was reluctant, he did come up to the front. As he stood next to me, I put my arm around him. I told him, "I need to ask for your forgiveness. I know I was inappropriate and was really upset last week, and I want you to know I am sorry, and I want you to forgive me."

He was shocked, but of course he accepted my apology. He also apologized for what happened, and we hugged right there in front of everyone.

Athletes in general are pretty selfish. It's hard to have friends and compete against each other. That is something I really had to work hard at after becoming a Christian. I had to learn how to be fair, not hurt people, and to put others first.

From Kyle Froman

"I hope you have a fire extinguisher with you, because I am coming to your chapel service today," one of the moms in our racing community jested as she walked past me.

A few years prior to this statement, I found myself in conversation with a racer in our community named Junior (not Earnhardt!). He had not been at a few of our more recent races, so when I saw him, I headed over to catch up with him.

"How are you doing, man? Whose car are you driving?" Junior asked.

"A rental," I replied. "I like to save the mileage on my car whenever I can!"

"Really? A rental?" He questioned. "And mileage? You are concerned with mileage on your car?"

"Well, yeah, I figure if I can save the wear and tear on my car, it will just last us longer. I always get great rates through my rental car account, so I figure, why not?!"

There was a long, awkward pause.

"I just thought you always raced your own car," he replied, somewhat puzzled.

Mistaken identity.

Junior had confused me with another racer in our community. This case of mistaken identity led to one of my first interactions with the aforementioned "racing momma." I had been mistaken for her son, and sharing this story with the two of them was one of the first icebreakers in what would become a long relationship with this family.

"I'll have the fire extinguisher right by my side!" I joked back as she walked on.

When the chapel service rolled around later in the afternoon, there she was, smiling, with two other members of their race team in tow. As we huddled from the noise against the NASCAR hauler, we spoke about God's epic love story with us, drawing comparisons from the PIXAR film *Finding Nemo*. It was a very foundational message about God's love for us, framed by John 3:16–17.

Following the chapel service, Racing Momma was quick to point out, "Well, the place didn't burn down!"

As she and her husband shared more of their back story, I learned that this was the first religious service she had attended apart from a wedding or a funeral in approximately thirty years. Having both been brought up Catholic, their angst at the hypocrisy of the church and the loss of their voice and identity within the church had led them to decide that they would never get back into the church again.

They had experienced a church that was full of requirements yet void of relationships. They found themselves face-to-face with people who could speak all about the responsibilities and rules of religion, yet who failed to live it in their day-to-day lives. They experienced the depth of a network of people who use God's name but who don't know Him. There was nothing personal and nothing authentic in the world they witnessed.

Yet they chose to come to a chapel service in the middle of a tiny speedway in Asheboro, North Carolina, amid the noise and distractions of a racetrack. They stood with twelve to fifteen other people in the open, beside the NASCAR hauler, praying, reading God's Word, and experiencing Christian community.

I had to know why.

She told me that they often watched me from a distance. They noticed me always talking to a lot of people . . . with a kind heart and a big smile. They also noticed that as my friendship with them grew, I wasn't in it to convert them or to convince them; I was in this friendship because I cared about them. I wasn't judging them, just loving them. They told me that they learned more from me just being myself in those moments of hanging out, than they had in any sermon they'd ever heard.

I was reminded of Zacchaeus. In Luke 19 we read about Jesus passing through the border town of Jericho on His way to Jerusalem. In Jericho was a chief tax collector named Zacchaeus, who had heard that Jesus was passing through. A big crowd formed, which kept Zacchaeus from being able to see Jesus. His only solution was to get some height, so he climbed to the top of a sycamore tree to see if he could lay eyes on Jesus.

As Jesus passed through, he looked up and said, "Zacchaeus, hurry and come down because today I must stay at your house" (Luke 19:5).

This was significant. It showed a relational side to Jesus' ministry.

Zacchaeus was not a popular man. In fact, tax collectors were hated by their fellow Jews, and often viewed as dishonest traitors. We know that Zacchaeus fell on the negative side of the spectrum because the crowd began to complain that Jesus had "gone to lodge with a sinful man!" (Luke 19:7). I love how *The Message* paraphrases verse 7: "What business does he have getting cozy with this crook?"

Yet Jesus called Zacchaeus out of his tree and invited Himself to Zacchaeus's home. He in essence said, "I want to spend time with you."

This wasn't the only time that Jesus was seen spending time with others in an effort to reach them with truth.

In Mark 2 we see Jesus lounging at a table at Levi's house. Also around the table were Jesus' disciples, as well as other sinners and tax collectors who were following Him. The teachers of the law couldn't handle it; they questioned Jesus' disciples on why He ate with such people. When Jesus overheard this, he replied to them, "Those who are well don't need a doctor, but the sick do need one. I didn't come to call the righteous, but sinners" (Mark 2:17).

Where do we see Jesus with these tax collectors and sinners?

In Matthew 9 we again find Jesus seated at the table in Matthew's house, with tax collectors and sinners joining Him and His disciples for a meal. Relationships were being formed around the table.

There is no doubt that Jesus valued relationships—it was exemplified in the way He lived. Yes, Scripture is filled with references to the gospel of God's grace being spread through teachings and proclamation, but we also have beautiful pictures of it being spread through relationships. Jesus could not have been accused of being "a glutton and a drunkard, a friend of tax collectors and sinners" (Matt. 11:19) if He was not in fellowship with "their kind."

In Scripture, you never see Jesus interacting with the "tax collectors and sinners" inside the temples or the synagogues. All His interactions happen, and all His relationships form, outside the walls of the church. This completely irked the Pharisees. They could not stand that Jesus was spending time with such people. This is another way that we know Jesus wasn't just preaching to the tax collectors and sinners. He was in relationship with them. The Pharisees could handle the sinners being "preached" to, but they could not handle a Messiah "getting cozy with those crooks" (Luke 19:7 *The Message*).

The truth is, relationships are a beautiful bridge to the gospel of God's grace.

Over the course of our marriage, my wife and I have spent countless Sundays at racetracks throughout the southeast in lieu of churches. Many weekends we've exchanged worship music, teachings, and potlucks for idling engines, conversations around stacks of tires, and grills on the beds of pickup trucks. To the Pharisees, we've skipped out on church for entertainment. But from our perspective, we're spending church time with the "racers and sinners."

This is a decision that can really irk the Pharisees.

Do you remember the two greatest commands we have as followers of Christ? The first is easy: love the Lord our God with all we have. We have to be "all in" with our love for Him. The second is a little more complicated: love our neighbor as we love ourselves (Luke 10:27).

The neighborly issue was a tricky one for the experts of the law to grasp. With an attempt at justification, they asked Jesus, "Who is my neighbor?" (v. 29).

Jesus responded with a parable, painting a stunning picture of love for one's neighbor—the catalyst of relationships.

He began by telling of a man who was heading down the road from Jerusalem to Jericho. To say that this seventeen-mile stretch of road was treacherous would be an understatement. The road's winding descent, surrounded by rocky terrain and caverns, made it an infamously dangerous, difficult passage. In Arabic, this throughway, about five miles outside of Jericho, came to be known as *tal 'at ed-damm* (which means "Ascent of Blood")[3] because of the bloodshed that often occurred as a result of robbers.[4]

As this lone traveler journeyed down the dangerous road, he was attacked by a band of robbers. The robbers stripped him of all that he had, leaving him beaten and half dead on the side of the road. Soon a priest approached, but upon seeing the man lying there, wounded and stripped, the priest passed by on the other side of the road, maintaining his distance.

Later, a Levite came along. Since Levites were servants within the temple, the Levite was a likely candidate to help the wounded man. Yet the Levite, like the priest, chose to distance himself and pass by on the opposite side of the road.

Finally, Jesus tells of a Samaritan who was journeying down the road from Jerusalem to Jericho. To Jesus' audience, this meant inevitable doom to the man on the side of the road, because in their world, with the tensions that ran between the Jews and the Samaritans, there was no way a Samaritan would stop to help this distressed traveler. The Samaritan would have categorically been another bad guy in this story according to Jesus' listeners.

However, to their surprise, the Samaritan not only had compassion for the man, he crossed over to where the man was and cared for his immediate needs by bandaging him. And the Samaritan didn't stop there. After meeting the stranger's immediate needs, he put him on his donkey and brought him to a local inn. He left the innkeeper with some money and asked the innkeeper to look after him and then pledged to return, assuring the innkeeper that any extra expenses would be covered as well.

Jesus then asked His listeners a question: "Which of these three do you think proved to be a neighbor to the man who fell into the hands of the robbers?"

"The one who showed mercy to him," was the response.

Then Jesus replied, "Go and do the same" (Luke 10:36–37).

What strikes me about Jesus' parable of the neighbor is that it paints a perfect picture of relationship. Loving your neighbor isn't a distant thing; it is a personal, intimate thing. Love requires action, service, and investment. We love our neighbor through relationship; it is our second greatest command.

How can we love our neighbor if we aren't going where our neighbor is?

If we truly believe Jesus' definition of a neighbor, going to our neighbor can be intimidating. Fear is a huge barrier to any relationship, but particularly a relationship with a neighbor.

We can only speculate as to why the Levite and the priest chose not to stop, but there is good reason to believe that fear is what kept them walking on. What if they stopped and the robbers were waiting for them as well? Or what if the man was dead and they risked becoming unclean themselves?

If it wasn't fear that kept the priest and the Levite away, maybe it was time. We all have schedules to keep, places to be and things to do. Could it be that these men passed by because they were too focused on making sure they kept their schedule with no distractions? One of the compelling traits of Jesus was that He always had time. He always had room in His agenda for interruptions.

Whatever the reason, the religious men in this parable didn't stop; they walked right on by.

We all have reasons not to go to our neighbor. We don't want to be associated with "that" type. We don't want to put ourselves at risk for someone else. We don't agree with their political or religious views. We don't want it to take away from our personal agenda . . . Our list could go on.

Martin Luther King Jr. said, "The first question which the priest and the Levite asked was: 'If I stop to help this man, what will happen to me?' But the Good Samaritan reversed the question: 'If I do not stop to help this man, what will happen to him?'"

To love our neighbor, we have to go to our neighbor.

Jesus did not instruct the disciples to set up camp and look for ways to draw people to them; rather, in Matthew 10 we see that Jesus sent them out to the lost (vv. 5–8). Just prior to sending the disciples, Jesus led by example. In Matthew 9:35 we read that Jesus was out in the villages and cities, teaching and preaching the gospel of the kingdom of God and healing sickness and disease among the people. He wasn't afraid of being seen with the sinners and tax collectors or of wearing the labels that people stuck on Him.

And what about Jesus' great commission to us before His ascension? "Go," He said (Matt. 28:19). Jesus did not call the lost to hear the gospel; He sent the gospel to be heard by those who need it.

We have to go to our neighbor, but the Great Commission doesn't stop there. In fact, it really just begins there. The second half of Jesus' commission was to make disciples and to teach them His way (v. 20).

Making disciples and teaching them Jesus' way is a personal, intimate journey. It requires service and it requires investment.

How can we love our neighbor if we aren't learning to serve our neighbor?

When the Samaritan saw the injured man's needs, he immediately acted to meet those needs. The Samaritan could have crossed over to the man, checked on him, and then continued on his way, but he didn't. He saw the need and met the need by tending to his wounds. The Samaritan served him.

In Matthew 5, as Jesus compares Christians to salt and light, we read: "Let your light shine before men, so that they may see your good works and give glory to your Father in heaven" (Matt. 5:16). Paul wrote in his second letter to Timothy that we "must not quarrel, but must be gentle to everyone, able to teach, and patient, instructing [our] opponents with gentleness" (2 Tim. 2:24–25).

In both passages we see that we have the ability to lead the lost to the gospel of grace through our action and interaction with them. How we serve them in their needs matters.

Last, how can we love our neighbor if we aren't willing to personally invest in them? After meeting the distressed traveler's immediate needs, the Samaritan didn't head off into the sunset like a superhero. Instead, he was in it for the long haul with this stranger, his neighbor. He took the time to transport this traveler to an inn and then paid the equivalent of two days' wages for his continued care. The Samaritan was committed to the wellness and healing of his neighbor.

When needs are presented, it is easy to get caught up in the moment of crisis and then move on with no long-term care for the person. We hear a heart-wrenching story or see a desperate need and we immediately want to do something. Our heart, or our pride, kicks in and we rise to the occasion, only to disappear afterwards, completely forgetting about the one we were serving. To truly be a neighbor is to invest in someone for the long haul.

My pastor and friend, Darren, is a beautiful example of someone who has committed to serve his neighbors for the long haul. Since 2007, Darren has been investing in and serving the people of Haiti physically and spiritually.

When the earthquakes struck the nation in 2010, Christians flocked to the Haitians' aide. Everyone was compelled to give and to get involved. Haitians were being served in the middle of their plight. But as time has passed, many of those immediate responders have come and gone, moving down the world's street to the next person in need and forgetting about the one they just had the opportunity to serve.

Darren has remained steadfast in his commitment to his neighbors. He has tirelessly engaged himself, his family, and our church community in serving and supporting these international neighbors. He is the first to say, "Social justice without Jesus is welfare. There's lunch, but no hope." But through his steadfast commitment to the "physical," he is entering into the spiritual with his Haitian brothers and sisters, exposing them to the gospel of God's grace—all because Darren is loving his neighbor.

We're not called to be ambulance chasers; love is a long-term commitment.

While our neighbor is everyone we come in contact with, those of us in MRO have chosen to personally invest ourselves in our neighbors in the motor sports community. We go to them, we serve them, and we invest in them. Maybe your neighbor is at your office or your gym. Maybe your neighbor is at your supermarket or involved with your children's Little League team.

Maybe your neighborhood is the military or the medical field. Whoever your neighbors are, you have to go to them. You have to walk across the street to where they are and serve them. It isn't about flying in and out; it is about making a long-term relational commitment to serve other people so that they can experience the gospel that sets people free.

We cannot love our neighbor or live in relationship with others if we are unable to overcome the obstacles of fear, time, isolation, and personal inadequacies. These are relationship blockers. Yet something beautiful begins to happen when we cross the street to where our neighbors are, when we take the time to get to know their needs and then serve them.

I remember sitting on the white painted wall of pit road at a short track where local racers were competing one extremely hot summer afternoon. As I sat with the sound of idling engines only feet away from me, another gentleman came and sat on the wall beside me.

He was someone I had not had many close interactions with. To be honest, he was someone who intimidated me. He had a reputation around the track as a tough guy, and I always perceived him that way as well. His look and posture fit the bill, so I never tried very hard to see what was behind that tough exterior.

The first few moments together on that worn, peeling wall were awkward. I wasn't sure if he sat there just to rest, or if he sat there because of me. After a few moments of silence (which is a very relative term for a racetrack), I made eye contact with him. Following another brief moment of awkward silence, he spoke.

"I watch you a lot," he said. "Everywhere you go there is glow around you. It is like you swallowed this light bulb and just shine as you walk around this place."

This gentleman did not have a relationship with God, nor did he care to. In his own words, he had been preached at and condemned enough by hypocrites. Yet now he sat by me in the middle of a racetrack, experiencing love and hearing about Christ. He allowed me this time because he saw me spending time with people. He watched from afar as I invested in people. He saw me imperfectly living my faith, and it affected him. He knew he wasn't just another patch on my vest. He knew I cared.

It wasn't long before the racing family I mentioned earlier found themselves in the middle of a very desperate trial in their lives, and my wife and I were by their side at 4:00 in the morning in a hospital waiting room. We weren't there because we wanted to convert them; we were there because we hurt with them and wanted them to experience the same hope that we have in desperate situations. We laughed together, we cried together, and we prayed together. Through it all, our friends were exposed to the true gospel of grace.

I could go on and on, filling the pages of this book with encounter after encounter with people who are so calloused from religion and the Pharisees that they cannot see God through their hurt. As we at MRO spend time with them in authentic relationship, sincerely loving them, those calluses peel away, exposing people who are raw for something more, revealing people who are in need of the hope of a Savior.

We should all be living in a way that compels people to follow Jesus.

Paul wrote in his second letter to the church at Corinth that in everything we do, we should show that we are true ministers of God. He went on to say that we prove ourselves by our purity and patience, our understanding and kindness, by the Holy Spirit within us and by our love (2 Cor. 6:4–6).

Chapter 9
Run Hard or Run Smart
Live with Patience

"You cannot give 110 percent. You cannot give 100 percent. The guys with patience, they give about 95 percent, and the other 5 percent is what they have in the tank."

From Darrell Waltrip

I'm that guy that says, "Oh, Lord, give me patience, but give it to me right now." That's how I am. But having patience in a race car is vital. You've got things inside of you that are raging, but you have to be able to control those emotions and not let them overcome good decisions.

We see it happen all the time with different drivers. They are really passionate about racing and winning, but they have a short fuse. They don't have any patience, and if you bump 'em or rub 'em the wrong way . . . it may be the first lap of the race, and they'll be mad the entire race, trying to get even with you!

That's another part of patience: you can't carry a grudge. Patience is so encompassing in the racing world. On the track, in the race, somebody's going to cut you off; somebody's going to make you mad. You have to pick your fights. You can't retaliate every time somebody does something you don't like. If so, you'll never win a lot of races and you'll never win a championship.

Jimmie Johnson is a very patient driver. Jeff Gordon is a very patient driver. They wait and watch. A lot of guys want to go and take it, make something happen. Guys with patience . . . they wait for it to come to them. And that's the difference. Impatient guys want to get it now—get it, get it, get it. That will get you in trouble. The patient guys, they say, "Yeah . . . go on out there and get at it. Boy, knock yourself out. Go on and beat your car up; make a bunch of people mad. At the end of the day, when it's all said and done, I'm going to be sitting here in position because I was patient and waited. When the white flag comes out, I can go hard and I have a chance to win!"

One of the worst things I hear people say is, "He gives 110 percent all the time!" In racing, that guy won't make it. You cannot give 110 percent. You cannot give

100 percent. The guys with patience, they give you about 95 percent, and the other 5 percent is what they have in the tank, held in reserve for the final run to the checkered flag. That is what happens when a driver like Kevin Harvick comes out of nowhere to win a race. He was patient and he waited.

Over time, the field thins out. When the race starts, you've got forty-two people you need to beat, but as the race goes on and the end of the day nears, cars drop out for different reasons and you may only have two guys to beat. Over the course of the race you let your team do its job, you let the pit crew do its job, you let the crew chief do his job, and now it's time for you to do your job—and now it's time for you to do your job and you have that extra 5 percent to give.

Every race has a set distance. If it is a 500-mile race, then it's not a 400-mile race or a 450-mile race; it's 500 miles. One of the hardest things some young drivers coming in today have to overcome is that they're used to running those races where really, truly, you can't have any patience. They come up through the ranks running local races where you have a thirty-lap feature, or maybe fifty and occasionally a hundred, and in these races you can't afford to have patience. As soon as the green flag drops, you've got to get all you can get. But when they start running NASCAR, this all changes, and like all of us, they have to learn what patience is all about.

One of my favorite sayings is, "Slow down and go faster." Just back it down, do it right, and then you only have to do it once. What's really bad is when we end up with everything messed up and we go back and say, "If I'd only waited. If I'd just been a little more patient. If I'd just taken a little more time."

From Billy Mauldin

One of the most exciting races in NASCAR is held every Memorial Day weekend in Charlotte, North Carolina: the Coca-Cola 600. What makes this race so special is the distance. There is not another race in NASCAR that is 600 miles. The most any other race goes—and there are a number of them—is 500 miles.

For a driver and the team, this distance presents a new set of challenges to both man and equipment. Engines have to last longer. So does the strength and mental focus of the driver. A driver once noted that the toughest thing about the Coca-Cola 600 is the reality that when you hit the 500-mile mark, you are usually at the point where most races are concluding. In the Coca-Cola 600, you are tired—yet you still have a hundred miles to go! Have you ever driven somewhere, ready to finally get home, only to realize you still have a hundred miles to go? It can be a bit demoralizing.

For every driver and team, the Coca-Cola 600 requires an extra level of patience. You want to get to the end of the race with your car in the best possible running condition—and yourself as fresh and focused as possible. This is true in every race, but the longer distance of the "600" makes it unique.

For one who is driven to win, patience can be a challenge. Things happen on the track that are beyond a driver's control. Sometimes drivers get caught in accidents caused by other drivers. Out of frustration, drivers will also try and do things with their cars that they know their car is not capable of doing—like driving them too hard into the corner—and the results are usually disastrous.

> Patience is better than power, and controlling one's temper, than capturing a city. (Prov. 16:32)

Sometimes it may take a good part of a race just to get the car to perform like the driver and team need it to. Sometimes races start in daylight and end with the sun setting, which affects the track conditions and the handling of the car. As track conditions change, the driver has to wait for the car to adjust. Yellow flags, or "cautions," also come when drivers do not expect them, and this forces them to once again adjust to changing circumstances beyond their control. To "capture the city," or win in this case, they must remain patient.

These are just a few examples of issues drivers and teams face that force them to exercise patience. Every driver knows that in order to have a chance to win, he or she must be around at the end of the race. No driver ever won a race in the first one hundred laps. Some days a driver and team must simply recognize what they are capable of accomplishing and run for points and the season championship, not the win.

Ministering to others is often an exercise in patience as well. Relational ministry involves allowing others to become comfortable with you. We want to see people come to know Jesus. We want to see them transformed by the Holy Spirit. We want them to know and experience what we have but, the truth is, these types of relationships often require as much patience on our part as it does for a driver to complete 600 miles of racing and be in a position to win!

But if we hope for what we do not see, we
eagerly wait for it with patience. (Rom. 8:25)

MRO is blessed to be at the track week in and week
out with the communities we serve. As a result, we are
able to allow them the opportunity to not only hear us
but watch us, and often there is much more watching
than talking. Our ministry takes place in the workplace. When we go to the track or visit a race shop, the
men and women we are there to see are often working.
The time we can spend with them is usually short, and
therefore the conversations are brief. It's not necessarily
ideal, but it is reality. This means that relationships, and
the trust and respect that they require, are built over
time as a result of a number of interactions. It takes
patience!

Authenticity is something our world is searching
and longing for. A writer doing an article on father-
hood asked me recently what I felt was one of the most
important characteristics a father should have, and I
responded, "Authenticity." It surprised him at first, but
I went on to explain that children today are constantly
being "sold" something. From TV to radio to digital
media and their friends, kids are bombarded with the
best spin on everything out there. Even on Facebook,

where you are told you are "Friends" and "Liked" more often than not, kids only get the best impressions and not the whole story. If a child cannot see the real deal—authenticity—in his or her father, then where will that child see it?

It is the same thing in ministry. Whether young or old, we are all being bombarded with the best impressions that others can put forward. After a while we become cynical of everything and everyone, hungering for that which is real and true. As children of God and followers of Christ, herein exists one of our greatest opportunities. We have the opportunity to stand out just by being genuine human beings who have good days and bad days, highs and lows, and who still, through them all, choose to trust in and rely on God. People are hungry to see this, and deep down, many want to believe it is real. As we live with mission and purpose, we have the chance to shine brightly in a world darkened by doubt and disappointment.

> You are the light of the world. A city situated on a hill cannot be hidden. No one lights a lamp and puts it under a basket, but rather on a lampstand, and it gives light for all who are in the house. (Matt. 5:14–15)

If ministry is planting seeds, then patience is the water the seed needs to grow.

I enjoy counseling those who are looking for answers. Nothing is more satisfying than to have someone come to you who genuinely wants help. I have often found myself talking with a person for hours—and even days and weeks—about issues that they desire to overcome in their life. My heart is to see them changed the moment I first speak into their lives, but this is not always the case. Patiently I continue to remain available—talking, encouraging, and praying for the individual while God, over time, works in their heart and life.

When you invest a lot of time in someone and they do not respond right away, it can cross your mind to give up on them. I have said more than once, "I am done with this situation!" The truth is, I may have done all I can do to that point, but patiently I continue to pray and believe that God will do a special work in their lives. It may take days, months, or years, but I know this to be a fact: He worked on me for close to fifteen years before I believed in Him, and He is still working on me today! If He can be so patient with us, it should not be a problem for us to offer the same to the world.

Patience also allows you to see potential pitfalls before you get caught up in them. As I mentioned before, a big part of racing is having the patience over the course of a race to get to the end with a good car capable of winning. Accidents happen all the time on the track, and although patience will not always prevent accidents, it will go a long way in helping a driver avoid them. More often than not, it is the impatient driver who causes the accident. The patient driver—the one watching, not trying to do more than the car is capable of doing; the one listening carefully to his or her spotter and crew chief—is the driver with the best chance to avoid the accident. Patience will similarly help us all guard against pitfalls in our personal lives as well as in our ministry to others.

In my zeal to see God do something in another person's life, I have occasionally gotten ahead of Him. This is my most common downfall. I like to tell people what they need to know and do, when sometimes the best thing I can do is just listen. Their need is to just be able to talk, to be heard. They often even know the answer to their own questions, but they need the time and opportunity to speak things out.

Over the years I have worked hard at becoming a better listener and allowing the Holy Spirit to guide me as to when it's time to talk. More often than not I have learned that this tack, which involves patience, results in successful ministry with fewer words spoken. God has a way, in His time, of dealing with the heart of a matter, and He gives us the knowledge and wisdom, as well as the opportunity, to be used by Him to help others who He loves dearly.

> Therefore, God's chosen ones, holy and loved, put on heartfelt compassion, kindness, humility, gentleness, and patience, accepting one another and forgiving one another if anyone has a complaint against another. Just as the Lord has forgiven you, so you must also forgive. Above all, put on love—the perfect bond of unity. And let the peace of the Messiah, to which you were also called in one body, control your hearts. Be thankful. (Col. 3:12–15)

People can also change for the worse and you have no idea what happened. There are times when we find ourselves in a relationship with someone who does not know Jesus but they appear to be getting more excited about knowing Him. This motivates us because we believe the moment is coming when they will give their lives to Jesus. We pray for them and talk with them.

We get hopeful and long to see them pray with us to accept Jesus as their personal Savior. Then, out of the blue, they want nothing to do with us! They avoid us. They distance themselves. They seem cold toward us. We can become frustrated and, if we're not careful, we can even grow angry at them. It is at this moment that we can cause a bigger and more devastating crash than NASCAR has ever seen, if we are not patient.

What's often happening in these times is that the individual is under attack from Satan. He is trying to steal the truth you have been exposing this individual to. He is trying his best to derail the salvation process.

> Be serious! Be alert! Your adversary the Devil is prowling around like a roaring lion, looking for anyone he can devour. (1 Pet. 5:8)

Former MRO chaplain Dale Beaver called this moment "The Cost-Conscious Factor." In ministering to nonbelievers and leading them to Christ, you might as well factor in the possibility of a moment when the enemy will flood their mind with thoughts of what they may lose if they choose to follow Christ. Satan causes them to question such things as, "Will I lose all my friends?" or "Could it cost me my job or livelihood?" or "What will my family think of me?" Any of a thousand questions will flood their minds in this situation, and they may actually grow scared of the decision to follow Jesus.

Your patience at this moment can make the difference. You need not become offended by the distance they put between themselves and you. You need not try to fix them. More than ever, they need to witness your love and belief in them, and they need your prayers as they are being sifted! Remember Jesus' words to Peter . . .

> "Simon, Simon, look out! Satan has asked to sift you like wheat." (Luke 22:31)

Patience is a fruit of the Holy Spirit and in these critical situations, we need God's Holy Spirit leading and guiding us as much as ever. Now this is really good news! The patience we need in ministry is really not even our own! It is the fruit of the Holy Spirit!

> But the fruit of the Spirit is love, joy, peace, patience, kindness, goodness, faith, gentleness, self-control. Against such things there is no law. (Gal. 5:22–23)

Patience is a gift from God to us. The patience of God manifested through us by His Holy Spirit is what we long for and need! The only thing we must do is submit ourselves to His Holy Spirit and allow that spiritual fruit to manifest in our lives.

When it comes to ministry, you have to be in it for the long haul. At MRO we always encourage those getting involved in ministry of any type to give themselves at least three years to determine how it will go. We tell them: The first year you will learn a lot about the people and the community you are being led to serve; you will learn about yourself and your gifts and talents; there will be many positive trials and errors—all further defining your calling.

The second year the community you serve will watch to see if you are really hanging in there with them. They will watch to see how consistent and authentic you are. They will watch how you manage your own trials to see if you really believe and do what you say. As all of this is going on, if you handle it all with patience, they are growing to trust and respect you.

The third year they really begin to open up and engage you. Through small talk or more deep and intimate discussions, you begin to experience what you have prayed and longed for: fruitful ministry. In fact, you will find yourself hearing unexpected stories of how different individuals have already been impacted by God through your presence! Patience has sustained you through lean times—the early years, if you will—and now patience is guiding you through the harvest!

> I solemnly charge you before God and Christ Jesus, who is going to judge the living and the dead, and because of His appearing and His kingdom: Proclaim the message; persist in it whether convenient or not; rebuke, correct, and encourage with great patience and teaching. (2 Tim. 4:1–2)

You have to be there at the end to have a chance to enjoy the win. You need to have "5 percent left in your tank." Every driver and team knows this! So "run smart" and practice patience. Together, those strategies will play a significant part in getting you to the end of the race where you will experience your own "Victory Lane" in ministry!

Chapter 10
Remember the Prize
Live with Fortitude

"Overcoming adversity is a character trait that true winners have. Not everyone can do it, but those who do are the ones who win the races."

From Darrell Waltrip

I won my first NASCAR Sprint Cup Series Championship in 1981, adding twelve wins to my name. To prove it wasn't a fluke, I backed up that first championship with a second one—and twelve more wins in 1982. Over the next three years I picked up sixteen more wins and sixty-six top ten finishes, racing my way to a third NASCAR Sprint Cup Series Championship in 1985. I had become the center of attention in NASCAR; I was at the peak of my career.

In 1986 Rick Hendrick approached me about driving for his team the next year. (At the time I was driving for Junior Johnson.) Rick and I had gotten to know each other personally through the car business. He had played a big role in helping me get my own car dealership off the ground in Franklin, Tennessee, and through it we'd become friends. Rick was a newcomer to NASCAR, having formed his team just a few years prior, and now he wanted me to be a part of what he was doing.

Following my conversation with Rick, I figured it would be the perfect time to attempt to renegotiate with Junior for the upcoming season. Those negotiations didn't go quite as I expected, and it soon became apparent that Junior and I would be parting ways at season's end after six successful years and three NASCAR championships together. The road was paved for me to join Rick Hendrick in 1987 as part of his "dream team."

During our first year together, our dream team had anything but a dream season. Waddell Wilson had been brought on as an engine builder and was essentially running our team. Initially, I was excited about working with him, but my excitement quickly wore off as we began to clash on nearly everything from the start. As the season drudged on, I was in jeopardy of having my first winless season since 1975. Following the tremendous success I'd had with Junior, it was a frustrating year on the track.

Off the track, Stevie and I were expecting a child. Stevie had three prior miscarriages—the most recent being in 1986—so we had some personal anxiety too. As the pregnancy progressed, Stevie could no longer come to the track with me. She had always been my rock at the racetrack; she was with me there before women were accepted in the pits. We'd always been together in this deal. So my challenging year became a little more challenging without Stevie by my side.

On September 17, 1987, our baby girl, Jessica, came into the world, ten days before our race in Martinsville, Virginia. I'd won at Martinsville a few times before, but I didn't feel like we had a shot of ending our drought this time around. I spent most of the race a lap down; however, a late pit stop by the leader helped me get back on the lead lap. As the race wore on, with about seven laps to go, I found myself running in third right behind Terry Labonte and Dale Earnhardt after a late race caution. Dale and Terry were both tough competitors, and there was no way I was going to get around both of them with just a few laps remaining.

When the green came out with three laps to go, Terry was all over Dale. They were beating and banging on each other ahead of me. On the final lap, Terry tried to pass Earnhardt on the outside through turns one and two. When Terry got to the outside of him, Dale drove him right up out of the corner and pinched him to the backstretch wall.

After the season I'd had, I was determined to take advantage of this battle. They both got a little sideways as they fought, and I was able to make it down inside of Terry heading into turn three. When I got there, I bumped into Terry and he hit Dale, and it sent them both up the track. I was able to get around them and just edge out Dale to end my winless streak with my new team.

What made the day even more special was, just prior to the race, I found a rose in the seat of my car that said, "Win one for me, Daddy."

My determination on the track carried us through that season and to that win in Martinsville. And off the track, Stevie and I were celebrating another victory: our resilience carried us through the heartache of three miscarriages, and now we were rejoicing in our beautiful baby girl.

Overcoming adversity is a character trait that true winners have. Not everyone can do it, but those who can are the ones who win the races.

From Kyle Froman

Just a few miles from the skyline of downtown Winston-Salem sits what is arguably one of the fiercest coliseums in America. Nestled into the campus of Winston-Salem State University is a tiny bullring of asphalt that encompasses the university's football field. Around the circumference, a red-and-white metal fence circles the pavement, marred and bent by grinding metal and fierce collisions. The feeble fencing acts as a barrier that separates the paved, storied battlefield from the concrete grandstands, which seat seventeen thousand people.

Every Saturday evening from spring until fall, this coliseum comes alive as loyal fans fill her to capacity to cheer on their favorite gladiators. In front of them, men and women fearlessly strap themselves into their hand-forged chariots and roll out onto the tiny quarter-mile track for battle. As the race cars come alive, the small bowl that is Bowman Gray Stadium erupts with the high-octane rumble of motors.

An undeniable tension accompanies the race cars as they claim the track. Each car has its own stories to tell. The wrinkled fenders, chipped paint, mismatched bumpers, and rubber-marked doors tell of previous battles and speak of future struggles. The competitors behind the wheels are stoic, focused, and prepared as they enter their battlefield.

The racing that unfolds on this tiny oval of asphalt is nothing short of physical. Men and women have to fight for every inch of pavement. There is very little give at Bowman Gray Stadium, and a whole lot of take. The rivalries that form can become bitter and flow very deep. Competing there is not for the faint of heart.

Almost as deafening as the sound of the engines is the roar of the crowd. Some of the most passionate race fans I have ever encountered are within this small coliseum in Winston-Salem. Much like the gladiators they show up to cheer on, they live and breathe for the spectacle that unfolds in this grand place. Their loyalties are deep, defending their favorite driver as if it were their own mother or father behind the wheel. It doesn't take long for competitors to know where they stand with the followers in the stands, as both obscenities and admiration fill the air, depending on the circumstances.

Lap after lap, racers who are despised by rival fans face a barrage of single-digit waves from the crowd as they circle the stadium. Upon their introduction, distasteful words reverberate through the stands, and upon their misfortune on the track, raucous celebration ensues.

It takes fortitude to race at Bowman Gray Stadium.
Yet week in and week out, racers strap into their
cars to do battle on this famed old track. Since 1947
it has been home to legendary automotive battles. The
racers who face off in this tiny bullring know that it is
demanding physically, mentally, and emotionally. Yet if
they hope to win at Bowman Gray, they have to push
on. They cannot let the challenges that accompany racing at that stadium deter them.

Those who win at Bowman Gray proceed with fortitude, unhindered by adversity.

We have to face a life on mission as we run our race
with the same resilience and determination.

In 2008 I remember a particularly soggy stretch
of weekends for the NASCAR regional racing community I was serving. Two of our first four events were
washed away by persistent rain in the southeast. If you
spend much time around motorsports, you will soon
learn that the quickest way to end a drought is to build
a racetrack. It seemed as if we couldn't catch a dry
weekend.

As my wife and I looked over our budget, preparing
for our fifth straight weekend on the road, we faced
the grim realization that we did not have the funds to
make it to the race. Along with the fund shortage, the

extended forecast for the weekend again showed rain on race day. We were conflicted.

After talking it over between ourselves and with God, we decided we would load up the car and head to our next event anyway, funds or no funds. At that, we headed toward Asheboro, North Carolina, with a plastic card in our pocket that we intended to charge our expenses to. I can again feel the Dave Ramsey faithful wincing, but we felt we needed to push forward in spite of adversity, and we really had no other means of doing so.

It didn't take long for the rain to find us again.

As the rain began to pour, a feeling of discouragement filled the pit of my gut. Not only was I disappointed that we had decided to make this trek without the funding to do so, only to have the event rained out, I also felt like I had missed the mark in pushing through despite the adversity we were facing.

Through the rain we walked (okay, we ran) down pit road to the NASCAR hauler so that we could get an official word on the fate of the weekend. As we stepped up into the trailer, there was a NASCAR official waiting for us.

"Has Mark found you yet?" he asked. Mark was our NASCAR tour director.

"No, we haven't seen him," I replied.

"Stay here," he said as he immediately radioed to Mark. "I found them."

That sickness in my stomach began to churn even more. Visiting a NASCAR director at the NASCAR hauler is the equivalent of being sent to the principal's office. Most of the time, invitees are not brought into that sacred meeting place without due cause. We knew Mark well, and he was a great advocate of MRO at the track, but in the sternness of the moment we could tell that something was up.

As Mark's red truck pulled up to the back of the trailer, he hopped out and ran through the rain to the trailer where we were, with something tucked under his arm. It was a thick, worn manila envelope that had seen better days. Without the customary pleasantries, Mark began to talk. As he spoke, he was animated and passionate with his gestures, yet still clutching the envelope tightly.

He told us that not long after the garage had opened that day, one of the racers in our community felt compelled to do something for Michelle and me. Of his own accord, he grabbed an old manila envelope from the back of his trailer and went from hauler to hauler, asking his fellow competitors to drop something in the envelope for us. After being sure everyone had the opportunity to give, he took it to Mark and asked him to pass it along to us anonymously, on behalf of our racing community.

As the rain continued to pour, I was speechless. Not one other person besides Michelle and I knew the state of our finances for that event. That's when I realized: this trip wasn't about the community; this trip was about us.

Because of our financial situation, we had been keeping a very tight watch on every penny we spent. We knew exactly how much we were going into the hole for this particular event.

When we made it to the hotel, still wet from the track, we dumped that worn old envelope into the middle of the hotel bed. As the checks, bills, and change cascaded onto the comforter, we were again overwhelmed. We must have counted through the gift three times. The total in the envelope was within dollars of our exact expenses for the weekend.

In His own way, God was teaching us that in spite of adversity, we should always continue to push forward in our race of sharing the gospel of God's grace with others. It was about obedience to our commitment and to our calling. As we faced the test of if we were "all in" for the cause of Christ, or if we would back away at our first trial in ministry, God reminded us that He was with us and would "work together for the good of those who love God: those who are called according to His purpose" (Rom. 8:28).

Our trial was small, but the impact was profound. We would face adversity, and we had to make the decision to push forward in spite of it.

As racers at Bowman Gray Stadium and around the nation have come to learn, you will not win without overcoming adversity. If drivers are unwilling to accept that challenges are ahead, and they are unable to push through them, the chances of hoisting a trophy at the end of a race are minuscule. Champions know that challenges come, and in response they are prepared to push a little harder, work a little longer, and sacrifice a lot more.

As followers of Christ, we, too, have to understand that to win our race, we must be prepared for adversity and suffering. While our suffering in Western culture does not look the same as those early martyrs, or those who worship God underground in nations dotting the globe, we do need to be prepared for what we encounter.

We may not currently experience the persecution that many Christians around the world face, but

Christian intolerance continues to increase in the West. While I am very timid to even compare the two, the truth is, the gradual decline we are on will eventually lead to persecution. Prior to His crucifixion, Jesus intimately shared with His disciples that if they were a part of this world, the world would love them, but because He chose them out of the world, the world would hate them and it would persecute them as it had Him (John 15:19–20). Paul also reminded us that if we desire to live a godly life, we can expect to suffer persecution.

Aside from increasing intolerance, our call to follow Christ may bring about other kinds of suffering. Our comfort and finances may suffer as we invest in God's kingdom. I will never forget Darren, the pastor of our church fellowship, holding up one of the nine-dollar plastic chairs that we sit in as a church family every Sunday. As he shared about the impact our funds were having in the lives of others "globally" (globally and locally), he reminded us that we make sacrifices as a church (like cheap plastic chairs as opposed to plush comfy ones) so that we can continue to be a conduit of God's grace and resources to others.

Sometimes it is relationships that suffer. While my wife and boys are behind our ministry 100 percent, sometimes they suffer by Daddy being away, and I suffer by being away from them. There are little missed moments that can never be replaced or relived. What's more, for the first five years of our ministry within motorsports, my bride was always by my side, traveling with me. As our lives transitioned and we welcomed children into the world, her role in our ministry shifted and we have spent a lot of nights apart. We have counted the cost, and it is worth it. But that doesn't make it easy or fun.

Sometimes it is our emotions that suffer. Sometimes it is our health and energy. Regardless of how we ache, we know that suffering and adversity will present themselves in any race. We have the choice to race with fortitude or to bow out prematurely.

The reason that racers push on in spite of adversity is that they know what they are racing for.

In 1992 the NASCAR Sprint Cup Series witnessed a true underdog story as an independent owner/driver catapulted himself into the national spotlight by winning the series championship. Alan Kulwicki came onto the scene in 1985 with no backing, one race car, and a low budget, but ready to compete against the top teams in NASCAR.

In 1988 Kulwicki accomplished the unthinkable with his modest equipment and budget, winning his first race in NASCAR's premier series at Phoenix International Raceway. As he continued to leave his mark on the sport, offers began to arrive from top teams who wanted Kulwicki to drive for them. Knowing he would continue to face obstacles and challenges on his own, he chose to push forward toward his goal of independently winning a championship as an owner/driver.

Kulwicki recognized and embraced the challenge. In November of 1992 he unloaded his number 7 Ford Thunderbird with the *Th* removed. Racing with *underbird* across the front of his car, he took to the track as the true underdog in a season-ending race with six drivers in contention for the championship. Facing the giants of NASCAR, Kulwicki rose above the opposition to claim the title of champion.

He knew what he was racing for, and to him it was worth the price to win the prize. If we hope to race to win in spite of adversity, we, too, have to remember what we are racing for. Paul reminded us in his first letter to the church of Corinth that we also race for a prize, and it isn't one that will fade away. We compete for an eternal prize (1 Cor. 9:24–25).

As Alan Kulwicki set out on his journey to become a Cup champion, he knew that trials lay ahead of him. It wasn't *if*; it was *when*. James painted that same picture for us in our faith journey. As he wrote to the twelve tribes in his letter, he began with "*Whenever* you experience various trials . . ." (James 1:2, italics added). As followers of Christ, we *will* face trials.

James goes on to shape what our response to these trials should be. Alan Kulwicki openly accepted the challenges before him, refusing to join bigger teams and choosing to persevere as an owner/driver. We can see through his proclamation of "underbird" that he embraced the suffering in pursuit of becoming a champion. He likely did not embrace the challenges because they were pleasant but because he had perspective regarding the rewards he could achieve if he persevered. He could face his trials with joy because he knew the victory he was racing for.

Suffering is just that. It's certainly not fun. So how do we find joy in the middle of our suffering? We are able to find joy through perspective. James reminds us that if we endure the trials, we are blessed, because when we pass the test of life, we "will receive the crown of life that God has promised" us (James 1:12). It may not be pleasant or comfortable now, but we have to remember that we are not racing for comfort now; we are racing for the win. We know that some temporary discomfort is worth it to obtain the crown of life God has promised to those who endure.

I am reminded of Daniel. Daniel was a faithful man with an extraordinary spirit. Within ancient Babylon, where Darius was king, the 120 satraps (governors) who oversaw the kingdom reported to Darius's three commissioners, one of whom was Daniel. On the king's corporate ladder, Daniel had become the standout. As such, Darius planned to establish him to rule over the entire kingdom.

The other commissioners and governors were not on board with King Darius's plan, so they came together in an attempt to unearth some political scandal that they could use against Daniel to change the king's mind. What they discovered was that Daniel was completely trustworthy, and there was no corruption in him. Undeterred in their cause, they conspired to find something against Daniel in the only way they could: by positioning the law of the king against the law of Daniel's God.

The government officials came to the king, hyped up his ego, and then presented him with a decree that stated that anyone who prayed to any god or human other than King Darius during the following thirty days would be thrown into the lions' den. They encouraged him to make the decree unalterable and irrevocable. Sold on their idea, the king signed the decree.

Upon learning about the decree, Daniel returned to his room and did as he had always done: he prayed three times a day, giving thanks to God. He knew the risk that was involved; he knew the suffering he would endure; yet he pushed through it because he had the greater race in view. He counted the cost of the suffering and knew it was worth it.

Of course, the conspirators found Daniel praying and immediately went to the king. When Darius acknowledged the decree and the fact that it could not be repealed, the group offered up their report about Daniel's continued prayers to his God. The king was distraught—Daniel was his chosen man, but now he was roped into an irrevocable decree. Under the pressure of the other officials, he made the order for Daniel to be thrown into the lions' den.

We all know how the story ends. When the king returned the following morning, he shouted with anguish to Daniel,

> "Servant of the living God . . . has your God whom you serve continually been able to rescue you from the lions?" (Dan. 6:20)

Yes. God had sent an angel to shut the mouths of the beasts. The "underdog" looked beyond the challenges of running the race well and focused only on winning the race.

We often stop there and forget to keep reading what is one of the most important elements of the story in Daniel 6. King Darius wrote to all the nations,

> May you prosper greatly! I issue a decree that in every part of my kingdom people must fear and reverence the God of Daniel. "For he is the living God and he endures forever; his kingdom will not be destroyed, his dominion will never end. He rescues and he saves; he performs signs and wonders in the heavens and on the earth. He has rescued Daniel from the power of the lions." (Dan. 6:25–27 NIV)

Admittedly, our perseverance in suffering is for ourselves. We grow in patience, character, and hope, obtaining the crown of life. But our suffering is also for others. If we are to be salt and light to the world around us, then how we respond to trials illuminates Christ to those who are watching. People will experience the gospel of God's grace through our persevering response to suffering.

Chapter 11
Boots, Hats, Ties, and Chrome
Live with Style

"Some people go down the paths of least resistance.
I go down a path that I can least resist!"

From Darrell Waltrip

I'm a car guy, and I've always been a car guy. I remember growing up in Owensboro, there was this guy with the ugliest car in town—an old, beat-up '57 Chevy that had bad paint. But when he put a set of chrome wheels on it, that car looked good! People started referring to him as "Tom with the '57 with the chrome wheels."

Chrome has always been one of my passions, but then, I'm a clean freak. Chrome is easy to keep clean. You know . . . you can wash it and shine it and polish it and it looks good. Since I'm fanatic about details, I would get a toothbrush and clean out a corner of a room so when you looked at it you say, "Man, this place is spotless!" That's just how I've always been. And so chrome fit me because you can actually make it spotless.

In 1997, to celebrate my twenty-fifth anniversary in NASCAR, I decided I wanted a chrome car! At first they said it couldn't be done. But I was watching a Formula 1 race and somebody had a chrome helmet. I thought, *How in the world did they do that? How'd they chrome that helmet?* So I went to our race shop that next week and said, "I want to chrome my car."

They said, "Well, that' ridiculous . . . you can't chrome a car."

I said, "Well, I don't know if you can or not, but we're going to figure out a way to do it."

I ended up with the first car that was ever wrapped instead of painted.

The only way you could do it was to wrap it, which is basically covering the entire car with a decal. Today they do it with all the cars, but that year we wrapped my car in chrome and then we detailed it with hot red—not just red but *hot* red! It was number 17 . . . my Western Auto car.

Then they said, "Well . . . you can't race it! In the rules it says you can't run anything reflective."

I said, "You just get the car wrapped in chrome and I'll take care of the rules."

I showed up at the Daytona 500 with my chrome car, and that thing was magnificent!

Dale Earnhardt Sr. and I got into a "chroming" contest one year on our Nationwide cars that we were taking to Daytona. I was the chrome king! Dale wanted to have a car that was better than mine, so every time I'd chrome something . . . he'd chrome something. By the time we got to Daytona, I had chromed tailpipes. I had chromed pedals. I chromed everything I could get my hands on. Anything you could remove on the car I chromed. When it came down to it I beat him because I had chrome jack stands and a chrome jack, and he didn't!

I never won anything in that contest, but it looked good!

In NASCAR you're in a world where you want to be seen. You want to differentiate yourself, and there are ways you can do it right. When I started in this sport, all you got for winning the championship were cowboy boots and big belt buckles! It was the prize and it was like a rodeo—big belt buckles, cowboy boots, and a big cowboy hat. It was sorta the dress code, if you will.

I came in to NASCAR and I wore loafers, button-down collars, slacks (not jeans) . . . and I looked for opportunities to be different. I wanted to be able to talk well. I wanted to look good. Now you can get into problems with some of these things if you become really consumed by them. For something to really work, it has to be natural. You can't pretend, and people don't like fakes. Nobody wants to deal with some guy who's fake. It was just my natural tendency to look at situations and go the other way.

When I did my NASCAR Hall of Fame Induction speech, I said, "You know, some people go down the paths of least resistance. I go down a path that I can least resist!" And that's what set me apart from the day I showed up.

It can be a haircut or a hairstyle. It can be the way you dress. It can be the way you look or the way you talk. I always think you have to look at who you are and what makes you unique and capitalize on it, especially when you are in a crowd.

In NASCAR, we are in a crowd and putting on a show, so our situation is a little different than if you're working in an office somewhere. But even in an office, if you show up every day and you wear a coat and tie while everybody else wears jeans or a pullover, you do that because you think that's the professional way to look. People are going to recognize you. They will say, "What about Bob? He comes to work every day wearing a coat and tie . . . what's up with that?"

"Who's Bob?"

"He's the guy with the coat and tie."

In that case, you have caught people's attention for the right reasons and you are being yourself.

It may be a hat, or your shoes. Some people may say, "I don't know about that guy. He wears those flip-flops everywhere he goes." There's a guy at our church who wears Bermuda shorts year-round. Wintertime . . . it can be 20 below and he shows up in church with a pair of Bermudas on. Strange to some, but that's what he does; that's just who he is.

It is possible to go to the extreme, drawing too much attention to yourself, but style—that's important. So ask yourself: *What is my style? What do I like? What do I do that is uniquely me?* This is your personality.

I think all of us look for an identity—some way to separate us from everybody else. And that's not a bad thing. I think God gives us all a unique personality and we're not to run from it. We're to embrace it. I embrace who I am; I'm not ashamed of who I am. I think one way or another we're all trying to impress somebody.

Being comfortable with who you are, knowing who you are, embracing who you are, not being ashamed or embarrassed by who you are . . . those are great traits of a confident Christian. So go get you some chrome and get busy!

From Billy Mauldin

A few years ago I was walking down pit road just prior to the start of a NASCAR Nationwide race in Nashville. All the teams were busy getting ready. Setting up their pit boxes. Preparing the surfaces where the cars will pit. Testing air wrenches and jacks. Huddling and talking strategy. It is an amazing thing to watch. At the same time, you can feel the intensity in the air beginning to grow.

As I passed the pit for number 3, I heard someone shout at me, "Billy!" I spun around and it was a crewmember named Hacksaw. Hacksaw said, "Come here!" So I walked over, not having a clue what was on his mind. We sat down on the pit wall together.

Now typically, what will happen in a moment like this is someone will start sharing some issue that is going on in their life. Problems with their marriage or their children. Maybe issues at work where they are not getting along with other crewmembers. It could be one of a dozen different things. But this time I got a question I wasn't expecting.

Hacksaw looked at me and asked, "Billy, why do you always wear those boots?" In my mind I thought, *What? You have watched me closely enough to recognize that I wear pretty much the same boots all the time.* But I immediately responded, "So I can tread on scorpions and snakes!"

He of course laughed, knowing that I was loosely referring to Scripture and the power our relationship with Jesus supplies.

Hacksaw and I went on to talk for another ten or fifteen minutes about his life, his faith, and all that God was doing in his life until it came time for me to head off and pray with the drivers before the race. I have never forgotten that moment. It reminded me of something I was taught years ago by MRO founding chaplain Max Helton. Max shared with me how he often carried a bottle of water in the front pocket of his shirt. It was as strange a sight to see at the track as anywhere else. And the reason he did it was because it drew people's attention. There is so much going on at the track, he said, that you sometimes have to make a little extra effort to get people's attention, and subtle elements of "style" can help you accomplish just that.

My own boots are far from fancy. In fact, they are just a plain brown pair of Justin cowboy boots made to work in. I don't even call them cowboy boots but refer to them as "plowboy" boots—boots that are made to get beat up and dirty. But at a racetrack very few people wear cowboy boots on pit road, at least not anymore (the exception being Richard Petty).

My boots are in no way intended to make a statement but they have differentiated me from others at the track and, as you've read above, they've opened the door for conversations. In ministry, especially in the workplace, that is what we are working toward. Sometimes standing out just a little can help make a way for those opportunities to talk with others.

If you stop and think for a moment, you can probably name half a dozen people or more right off the top of your head that are recognized by their style. In NASCAR alone there is Richard Petty and his Charlie 1 Horse cowboy hats. Jack Roush also sports the hats and has been nicknamed "The Cat in the Hat"! Staying with the theme and showing my age a little, I cannot help but think of legendary football coaches Paul "Bear" Bryant and Tom Landry, whose hats distinguished them from others. Little things like this set people apart from others and cause them to be quickly recognized.

In recent years I had the opportunity to host Franklin Graham at a NASCAR race, the Coca-Cola 600 at Charlotte Motor Speedway. Franklin was invited to give the invocation before the start of the race as well as speak in chapel for MRO. Once he arrived at the track, I met him in the parking lot to take him to lunch. When he stepped out of the car, I'm sure I had a bit of a funny look on my face as he stood there in a suit!

Now to see a Graham—Franklin or Billy—in a suit is not necessarily a surprise, but to see anyone in a suit at a NASCAR race is a bit of a shock! I quickly explained to him that he did not need to wear a suit, thinking he was doing it because he was speaking in our chapel. It was also probably ninety-plus degrees outside and extremely humid, and I knew he would be hot all day long. He told me, and these are his exact words, "My daddy would be very upset if I did not wear a suit when I preached!"

Okay, I am not one to argue with Franklin Graham, and I understand that it was a matter of respect to dress appropriately for the opportunity he had been given to serve God. It was what he and his dad both felt was the appropriate style, and on this day, I would soon see, it would serve him well in other ways.

After lunch I took Franklin and his guests down into the garage to see the cars and teams up close. As we walked, he was quickly seen and recognized by everyone; he didn't need to do a thing to be a testimony to the Lord, other than to be present. His personal presentation, inspired by his father and intended for no other purpose than to honor God, drew others to him, and more important, to the One he represented, our Lord Jesus Christ! That suit and tie caused him to stand out among literally tens of thousands of people at the racetrack.

There is another situation to consider that we're regularly involved in. Often we have the incredible opportunity to host the men and women of our Armed Forces for a day at the track. Part of their visit is a tour of the garage area, where teams are making final preparations on the cars and officials are conducting final inspections. Fans are everywhere, watching all the action, and the atmosphere is full of energy. Everything is building up to the start of the race.

It is not a secret that the NASCAR community has, and always shows, a great deal of respect for our military. We understand the sacrificial service they and their families provide for our nation, and we want to show them our appreciation whenever and however we can. In order to do this, I always ask them to come in uniform when they join me for a day at the track. Their uniforms do more than identify their branch of service. As soon as anyone in our community sees someone in a military uniform walk into our garage, that serviceman or -woman is noticed, identified, and invited to visit and see things related to racing that most fans would never have access to. He or she is also instantly welcomed into a more personal relationship without even saying a word. It is all expedited by the uniform.

I want to be very careful regarding this approach that we are sharing with you. As Darrell Waltrip shared above, we are not talking about being overboard to the point of flamboyant and self-promoting. Plenty of people have taken this tactic a bit too far in their desire to be seen and recognized. What we want you to see is simple gestures that will allow you to be seen in a world where it is easy to be missed due to busyness and the hurried lives we all live.

As believers and followers of Christ, we are called to be light and salt.

You are the salt of the earth. But if the salt should lose its taste, how can it be made salty? It's no longer good for anything but to be thrown out and trampled on by men. You are the light of the world. A city situated on a hill cannot be hidden. No one lights a lamp and puts it under a basket, but rather on a lampstand, and it gives light for all who are in the house. In the same way, let your light shine before men, so that they may see your good works and give glory to your Father in heaven. (Matt. 5:13–16)

As chaplains, our prayer and heart's desire is that people will see the Jesus in us. In this world, however, all followers of Christ will stand out, and it is the Christ in all of us that should be what people ultimately see. We at MRO have also learned that little things will help you get a little attention, especially if they are a part of who you really are. And for every Christian, those little things can be used for the purpose of directing that attention toward Jesus and not toward ourselves.

One of the greatest compliments I think I have ever received was one given to my wife and me while we were in college and still dating. One Sunday morning Julie and I stopped for breakfast at Hardee's just off campus. There an elderly man eating breakfast with his wife spoke up and said to us, "You guys are special; we can see God all over you both . . . you shine!"

Wow! What a compliment! In this case, there was nothing to identify us as Christians. We were just two college-age kids eating breakfast. In fact, I think we had skipped out of church early because we were hungry, but that morning God's presence, His light, shone through us and captured the attention of another couple.

On more than one occasion someone stopped Max to ask him why he carried that water bottle in his shirt pocket. For anyone who did not know Max personally, it was a simple, nonthreatening way to start a conversation. Max wanted people to talk with him; he wanted them to feel comfortable approaching him. He knew that first conversations are not always going to be about deep issues of the heart. People need a way to ease into those types of discussions, especially until they get to know you better and trust you. A silly thing such as a water bottle in Max's shirt pocket was like the doorbell on a home—it gave him the thing he needed to get strangers' attention and begin the process of building relationships. Such simple things can provide any of us with a simple way to engage others as we are trying to introduce ourselves. And hopefully this leads to deeper conversations about the issues of life that people struggle with—the issues they need a relationship with Jesus Christ to resolve.

Over time, people observe you as you live out your mission. In the beginning it may be your personal style that grabs their attention. But eventually they will recognize something in you and other believers that will draw them in—the presence and love of God!

"By this all people will know that you are My disciples, if you have love for one another." (John 13:35)

God's presence and love in our lives is amazing. In the end, nothing will draw attention to us—and ultimately to Him—like His love emanating from us! He pours His love into us by the Holy Spirit so that we can then pour it out through our words and actions to others. His presence covers us as we walk out our day-to-day lives, watching for the opportunities He provides to minister to others. To love others as Christ has loved us and to carry His presence into the world is a part of the mission we all have. It is also what causes us to stand out in a world fallen and struggling with so much hurt, pain, and confusion.

Your intentional efforts at building relationships with others may begin with simple conversations resulting from your own personal water bottle, or boots, or hat, or suit. Whatever you decide to do, make it a simple reflection of who God has made you to be. From there, others will see and discuss with you what they really need to come to understand—the thing that really sets you apart from the world: your personal relationship with Jesus Christ.

Chapter 12
Slow Down and Signal
Live with Your Actions

*"The most valuable sense you have
is your common sense."*

From Darrell Waltrip

It has been said: "You may be the only Bible anyone ever reads." That is so convicting to me. We all know we are far from perfect. We have weak moments when we say and do things we regret and wish we could take them back. My dear friend and first chaplain with MRO, Max Helton, put it this way: if you are in a room with other Christians and you are uncomfortable, then maybe you need to look at where you are in your relationship with Jesus. I think about that a lot. When I am in a group of people more biblical than I am, I can become self-conscious. It is important to me that I can be comfortable and relaxed in this type of setting because I have peace about my relationship with God.

Lake Speed, a friend and former driver I competed against, created a hand signal based on his belief that the Lord can never fill your "cup" if your cup is upside down (the cup being a symbol of our life and relationship with God). How can God give you any blessings if your "cup" is sideways or upside down. The idea arose because we were discouraged about drivers giving each other the "bird" or the fist during races. So the thought was, *How can we be encouraging to each other during the race when we cannot talk to each other?* That's when Lake came up with the "cup" idea. We would drive up beside each other right in the middle of the race, going 190 miles per hour, and if one of us was having a bad day, we would hold our hand, shaped like a cup, upside down. If we were having a good day, we would hold it right side up. This was a signal to each other that let us know how the other was doing. It was a signal to the other the need for prayer or to say that God was blessing me and I was thankful! To this day, you can flash the "cup" symbol to individuals in the garage and they will know exactly what you mean!

I grew up in an era when there was no radio communication, so we had to use hand signals to communicate with the pit and with other drivers. For example, if you put your hand out the window and hit on the roof of the car, that meant your car was loose. If you hit on the door, that meant it was pushing. If you hit on your helmet, that meant you needed a relief driver. Back then, all we had was signboards, but you try to read a chalkboard at 180 miles per hour!

In the car we also had signals for other drivers. If you made a motion with your hand like a chopping sign, it meant to stay in line. If you made a fist, it meant, "Hold what you got and just stay right where you are." If you pointed one way or another, it meant the direction you were going—left or right, high or low. Even today you will still see drivers put their hand out the window on a restart and tell other drivers to come by or thank them for letting them come by. There is a lot of nonverbal communication in racing even now.

When you are around people, you can tell by their body language whether they are down, discouraged, sad, or happy. Intuition—that sixth sense or gut feeling about what's going on around us—is something a lot of people are not tuned in to. That is how I do a lot of things. When I go to talk to a group and I walk into the room, they ask me, "Do you have any notes?"

No, I don't. I like to walk into a room and talk to the people and feel them out before deciding what I am going to talk about.

The most valuable sense you have is your common sense. I am not a real detail kind of person; I am a get-it-done guy. It is not always what is said that needs to be heard but what is observed. Actions can speak louder than words, so actions must always be considered. We must learn to be conscious of others' actions as well as our own. We also need to keep our "cup" full!

From Billy Mauldin

Such a person should consider this: What we are in the words of our letters when absent, we will be in actions when present. (2 Cor. 10:11)

It is moments before the start of a race. The invocation and the national anthem have just concluded and everyone has witnessed a spectacular flyover. All that is left is for the Grand Marshal to utter the most famous words in racing: "Drivers! Start your engines!"

Officials and security are busy clearing the grid of all the spectators, and drivers are making final checks as the track safety nets are being lifted and latched into place. Time is running out and I need to check with just a few more drivers before they roll away—drivers I did not yet have the chance to pray with.

Time is up! The famous words are spoken as the fans roar and the engines are fired. The noise becomes deafening and the opportunity to do any praying with anyone is now past. No one on the grid can hear a word anyone else is saying unless it is over a radio and headset. So what do I do? Time for hand signals!

The garage is hopping! It is the final practice before the race. Every team is working hard, making final adjustments on their cars, trying to get that perfect set-up for race day. Men and women everywhere are working hard, running to and from the team haulers as well as under and inside the cars. Tires are being checked and prepped. Drivers and crew chiefs are huddled up, talking strategy. A lot is happening and the environment is charged with energy. As a chaplain, you remain ever present to help, yet what can you do when you cannot speak to anyone and no one can stop long enough to talk?

As Darrell pointed out, in racing as in any other sport, there comes a time when nonverbal communication is the only option you have and hand signals are golden! In racing it is not unheard of to have a driver and crew chief lose communication due to a radio failure. When this happens, they cannot just stop and fix it for fear of losing laps and position on the track. They must wait till the next caution to pit and work on the issue. Until then, they must depend on hand signals to communicate.

At MRO we have learned over the years that a great thing to develop is quality nonverbal communication. There comes a time when words are just not possible but things need to be communicated and messages need to be received. We have also learned that our actions, more than what we say, are often what we are being judged by. Often we underestimate how closely we are being watched until someone mentions something they watched us do, and then we realize that indeed, others are paying attention.

A few years ago, then-MRO chaplain Tim Griffin shared in chapel about a dilemma we face as chaplains. People at the track are very busy and do not have time to stop and talk, yet we want to be there for them. He explained that we still love them and we want to remind them of that often. We also want to know when they need us to pray for them. So that day in chapel, he introduced a simple hand signal: tapping your heart with your hand. The understanding would be that if we, as chaplains, saw anyone direct that gesture toward us, it meant they needed us to pray for them. It would also become a simple signal of appreciation for the other party.

These days I continue to walk through the garage or down pit road prior to a race, when everything is crazy-busy and everyone is hard at work. It is not uncommon for me to share this gesture with someone across the garage working on a car, or a driver strapped in and ready to roll off onto the track, or an official who is hard at work yet thankful to know he is seen and recognized and being prayed for. More times than you would imagine, it is this simple gesture—or even just eye-to-eye contact—that lets me tell someone they are cared for and thought of.

For anyone who wants to have an impact on people's lives, it is good to become aware of the opportunity and impact that nonverbal communication can have on others. With simple gestures, intentional eye contact, a smile, even the way we walk, we "tell" people that they are important.

In the early morning hours as Jesus was being beaten and tried, Peter watched from a distance. Scared and probably a bit confused, he could not tear himself away, yet he could not allow himself to be associated with his Master, Jesus, who was being tried for crimes He did not commit. After being identified with Jesus three times by strangers, and three times denying that he knew Jesus, Peter heard the cock crow, and the words of Jesus from just hours before rang in his ears:

> "Tonight, before the rooster crows, you will deny Me three times!" (Matt. 26:34)

Peter had done it. He had just denied three times the Man he claimed he loved dearly—the Man he vowed to follow to death. And he'd let Jesus down when Jesus needed him most. Now what was he to do?

Every time I read of this scene in Scripture, I thank God He gave it to us in His written Word. Of all the instances of nonverbal communication in the Bible, this one stands out to me the most. The pain and agony Peter must have felt when he realized what he had done, even after being forewarned . . . His heart must have been broken. But the Bible records an amazing response from Jesus in another portion of Scripture:

> Then the Lord turned and looked at Peter. So Peter remembered the word of the Lord, how He had said to him, "Before the rooster crows today, you will deny Me three times." (Luke 22:61)

Jesus did not say a word; He just turned and looked at Peter. He looked at him!

What was Peter expecting? A look of hurt? A look of anger? A look of disgust? If I had just done what Peter did, I would not expect a look at all but rather, for Jesus to look away from me because that is what I so often do to people who betray me—I just turn away and refuse to have anything else to do with them. But not Jesus. Jesus had already told Peter that He knew Satan wanted to sift him like wheat. Jesus already knew Peter was marked for attack by the evil one. And Jesus had already told Peter He had prayed that his faith would remain strong.

As devastated as Peter was, and as wrong as his behavior was, Peter could not have seen anything other than love when Jesus turned and looked at him. Not a word was spoken. Just a glance that reminded Peter he was still loved. In the days following, when to all the disciples it appeared Jesus was dead and gone, that one glance would be all Peter had to hang on to. A simple, nonverbal glance that said, "I love you."

Living our life with purpose and mission means we must be conscious of every way we can possibly communicate with the people God puts in our life. Our actions can powerfully draw people to God, or instead reinforce in their minds some past misperception that was planted there by bad experiences or false teaching. Our actions, intentional or not, can be key to drawing people to Christ or providing reason for them to further disregard the need for a relationship with Him.

Another interesting Scripture is one where Jesus Himself warns those listening about showing favoritism to others:

> My brothers and sisters, believers in our glorious Lord Jesus Christ must not show favoritism. Suppose a man comes into your meeting wearing a gold ring and fine clothes, and a poor man in filthy old clothes also comes in. If you show special attention to the man wearing fine clothes and say, "Here's a good seat for you," but say to the poor man, "You stand there" or "Sit on the floor by my feet," have you not discriminated among yourselves and become judges with evil thoughts? (James 2:1–4 NIV)

In this case, the nonverbal communication is the attention given to others at a party. I cannot tell you how many times I have been talking to someone when, all of a sudden, they looked over my shoulder at someone else coming their way who they deemed more important. As soon as it happens, you feel like you should just move on, because you are now in the way.

I have worked hard to avoid making this mistake myself. I've learned to focus just on the person in front of me because he or she is the one God has opened the door for me to speak with in that moment.

Another thing I have learned to watch is how fast I walk. Now I know that sounds crazy, but there's a good reason for this. In the world of racing, people are going at an extremely fast pace (no pun intended). Much has to get done, and often in a short amount of time. The common understanding in NASCAR is this: if someone is walking fast, then they have somewhere to be and something to do, so leave them alone. And because everyone is pretty much moving like this, it's easy for us as chaplains to do the same.

But what am I here for? To be available to anyone who needs help. What I have experienced is that when I slow down—and I mean, intentionally walk slowly through the garage—people are much more likely to stop me and speak with me if they can. If I slow down, then they feel free to slow down and talk. If I am rushing, then they don't bother stopping me.

Many of us work in environments that are as busy and as active as a NASCAR garage. This is not something unique to our sport, so ask yourself this question: Can I slow down and open a door for someone to speak to me who normally would not want to bother me because I seem to busy? Can I walk a little slower down the hall, through the office, across the construction site in such a way that I am not only a little more approachable but also appear to be less hectic? Slowing down can be a powerful, nonverbal testimony of God's peace in your life and your availability to others.

As a family we Mauldins are fortunate to have the opportunity to go out almost every week and help feed the homeless in our city. The effort is led by a longtime friend, Daryl Sutherland. Daryl has done this for a number of years, and his approach is very simple: invite the homeless to come eat in the name of Jesus. Line up, let us serve you, let's hang out while you eat, and feel free to go on your way when you are done. There is no required Bible study or sermon before they are served. No rules or regulations about how often they can come. They just show up as they are and eat! It is beautiful!

In the time my family and I have been involved, we've had the opportunity to pray with a number of our special guests. They have come to know our children and my wife and me, and they know we love Jesus.

We will never forget the night our son gave a home-less man a set of brand-new guitar strings for his guitar. You would have thought he had given him a million dollars. The man looked at our son and said, "No one has ever done this for me." That simple act of kindness, extended by a child, demonstrated to a grown man that love can be unconditional.

In life, others are watching us as they try to deter-mine if they can trust us, especially if we publicly pro-fess to be Christians. It isn't always fair—and maybe we personally have done nothing to deserve such scru-tiny—but guess what? We live in a society where skep-ticism is rampant. By nature, people struggle to believe that others are capable of genuinely caring for them, so they watch. They judge our actions. They look to see if what we profess is consistent with what we do. They want to know they are getting the real thing, and the process involves us being as aware of what we do as we are about what we say.

We take it a step farther when we realize that who we are can more often be better understood and believed by others when we live and do with integrity. Our words are important, but so are our actions if we want to be intentional, nonverbal communicators who strengthen our witness for Christ.

Actions open the door for discussions. At times, actions are our only option for communication. So let's do some self-evaluation. What are our actions saying to others? Are we taking advantage of the power our actions have to communicate to others that they are valued, thought of, and loved?

In the place God has placed you, with the people He has given you to love on, start adding nonverbal communication to your daily interactions and watch what happens. They're likely to respond with curiosity and appreciation that you care enough to let them know, even when you cannot speak a word.

Chapter 13
Take a Seat and Let's Chat for a While
The Final Lap

From Billy Mauldin

I was blessed to know both my grandfathers. Each in his own way was a great man. They lived through difficult times, yet they worked hard and provided for their families. They also modeled faithful attendance to the things of the Lord, such as prayer, Bible study, and regular church attendance. As is the case with all of us, they were far from perfect—and would have been the first to tell you so—but they knew the Lord and they made sure their families were introduced to Him as well.

I also have vivid memories of something else they shared in common. They both had front porches where they would sit in the evening, after work and on weekends, to relax and watch as the world drove by. It was a common practice for the times they lived in. There was no air-conditioning in the house, so you had to get outside just to catch a cool breeze in summer if nothing else!

My father was the same way. He enjoyed sitting back in the shade of the porch and the cool of a breeze, just taking in the world around him as it went about its business. As a child I had many opportunities to sit with them all. As I look back, I wish I had done so more often.

In Philippians—a letter written later in life by the apostle Paul while in prison—we find this wonderful insight into where Paul had grown as a man, a minister, a leader, and a follower of Jesus:

> My goal is to know Him and the power of His resurrection and the fellowship of His sufferings, being conformed to His death. (Phil. 3:10)

I just love this verse, and I thank God He showed it to me many years ago. Like many of you, I spent time trying to decide what I was supposed to do with my life. How should I serve God? What was my calling? What purpose was I created for? Was I supposed to be a pastor or missionary? God, what do You want me to do? What have you prepared me for and what does my "race" look like?

All these thoughts would bounce around in my mind, especially as I watched others apparently find the answers for themselves while I felt as clueless as the day I first accepted Jesus as my Savior. But then one day I read Philippians 3:10 and the light of truth shined on and in me like never before. And I have never walked out of it.

In this verse I cannot help but see Paul as I described my grandfathers and father above: later in his years, sitting back on his front porch and reflecting on life. He was a man who had done just about everything imaginable for the Lord. A man who had experienced so much and was still facing incredible challenges and obstacles. The type of man we would all be wise to sit down with and ask, "Would you tell me what you have learned about life?" And as soon as we uttered the question, he would look at us without hesitation and say, "Make it your goal in life to know Him!"

My goal, my purpose, my calling, my mission, my race has all been revealed to me. It is to give myself to "progressively becoming more deeply and intimately acquainted with Him, perceiving and recognizing and understanding the wonders of His Person more strongly and more clearly" (Phil. 3:10 AMP). It is not an exercise to figure out what I am supposed to do. My race, our race, is to know Him!

Jesus also spoke to this in John 17 as He prayed in His final hours before His betrayal, trial, and crucifixion. In this prayer Jesus states:

> "This is eternal life: that they may know You, the only true God, and the One You have sent—Jesus Christ." (John 17:3)

Eternal life (not just *life*) is found and experienced in knowing God the Father and His Son, Jesus! Life is not about what we do. It is about who we know, and the only ones who truly matter are them.

Sometimes in life we need to just slow down and make sure we have the horse before the cart. When it comes to living and experiencing life as God intended, it begins with our never-ending pursuit to know Him. As we do, our lives are transformed into the image of Jesus. As transformation takes place, we learn to hear and follow God's leading through the gift of His Holy Spirit. And then, as we follow, we accomplish the mission that He has for each and every one of us.

He leads us and guides us. He provides and protects. Never again do we need to worry or be anxious about our mission in life. The Lord takes us where He wills and does with us as He pleases, and we have the incredible gift of living in His love, peace, and joy.

Every NASCAR race begins with the waving of a green flag. It is the signal to go! At that moment, all forty-three cars accelerate and the race is on!

Our green flag moment in life is when we accept Jesus Christ as our personal Savior. It is then that the real race of life—eternal life—is on! And at the moment that "green flag" waves, we need to step on the gas of our lives and head in one direction: straight into the arms of God! In His presence, in staying close to Him, we continue to grow in knowing Him for our entire lives. In knowing Him, we remain prepared to serve Him at any time, in any situation, however He pleases.

Take a seat on the front porch of your heavenly Father's dwelling place. He has created a spot just for you. Sit back and ask Him questions and let the Creator of life itself explain to you, show you, and prepare you for what your life is really all about. He is watching and waiting for us all.

So, are you a racer? Are you ready to run the race? Have you experienced the waving of the "green flag" in your life? Are you ready to be God's ambassador in this world? Are you ready to go? If so, then the goal we all share in common, the purpose for which we all exist, the mission we have all been created for, the race we run, is this: to know Him and to make Him known!

In the words of our good friend Darrell Waltrip, "Boogity, boogity, boogity! Let's go racing!"

Notes

1. Marty Smith, "JJ driving for third straight title; Knaus driven to make sure he gets there," ESPN, accessed June 15, 2013, http://sports.espn.go.com/rpm/nascar/cup/columns/story?columnist=smith_marty&id=3657183.

2. *Matthew Henry's Concise Commentary*, Bible Commentary, accessed June 16, 2013, http://www.christnotes.org/commentary.php?b=46&c=9&com=mhc.

3. *Luke 10—IVP New Testament Commentaries* at Bible Gateway website, accessed August 8, 2013, http://www.biblegateway.com/resources/commentaries/IVP-NT/Luke/Discipleship-Looking-Our-Jesus.

4. *From Jerusalem to Jericho* at American Bible Society website, accessed August 7, 2013, http://bibleresources.americanbible.org/node/1491.